· GALLIMAUFRY ·

Gallimaufry

A hodgepodge of our vanishing vocabulary

MICHAEL QUINION

OXFORD
UNIVERSITY PRESS

OXFORD
UNIVERSITY PRESS

Great Clarendon Street, Oxford OX2 6DP

Oxford University Press is a department of the University of Oxford.
It furthers the University's objective of excellence in research, scholarship,
and education by publishing worldwide in

Oxford New York

Auckland Cape Town Dar es Salaam Hong Kong Karachi
Kuala Lumpur Madrid Melbourne Mexico City Nairobi
New Delhi Shanghai Taipei Toronto

With offices in

Argentina Austria Brazil Chile Czech Republic France Greece
Guatemala Hungary Italy Japan Poland Portugal Singapore
South Korea Switzerland Thailand Turkey Ukraine Vietnam
Oxford is a registered trade mark of Oxford University Press
in the UK and in certain other countries

Published in the United States
by Oxford University Press Inc., New York

British Library Cataloguing in Publication Data
Data available

Library of Congress Cataloging in Publication Data
Data available

Designed by Jane Stevenson
Line illustrations by Robin Carter
Typeset in Centaur and Officina
by Alliance Interactive Technology
Printed in Great Britain
by Clays Ltd, Bungay, Suffolk

ISBN 0—19—861062—9   978—0—19—861062—5

Contents

Introduction

WHEN I WAS YOUNG—too many years ago to
want to remember but not yet so long ago to
want to boast about it—we used to catch trains
at a railway station. Anyone younger than about 40 will probably call it a *train station* instead. You can't fault the logic: if
you get on a bus at a bus station, why not a train at a train
station? It's a change that slipped into the language almost
without anyone much noticing it, imported from the American
term, itself relatively recent.

It's an example of one type of shift in our vocabulary, in
which names for things change under a variety of forces.
Others include the adoption of *duvet* in recent decades for
what in the 1960s—on the rare occasions we encountered
one—we would probably have called a **continental quilt**. We
seem similarly to have lost **off-the-peg**, to be replaced by
ready-to-wear. **Aerodrome**, once common, has been replaced
by *airport*; we now speak of the *radio* rather than the **wireless**;
bosoms seem endangered through the bold emergence of

breasts and *boobs*. Our harried lives lead to abbreviation: **brassière** has almost entirely been replaced by *bra*; **refrigerator** is a formal term, with *fridge* almost universal in everyday speech; **luncheon** has been shortened except in very formal situations (it's *ladies who lunch*, not *ladies who luncheon*, though you can still buy tins of *luncheon meat*). Many medical terms have been changed for various reasons, so that **infantile paralysis** is now *poliomyelitis* or *polio*, terms that themselves are becoming rarer now that the disease has been eradicated from most of the world; the wasting disease **consumption** is usually called *tuberculosis* these days, or just *TB*. When we joined it, the group was called the **European Economic Community** (**EEC**), or informally the **Common Market**; now we must call it the *European Union* (the *EU*).

Sometimes the opposite happens and the technology changes but the language doesn't. In Britain we still often speak of **telegraph poles**, even though the telegraph has been dead technology for a century; we still **dial** a telephone number, though virtually all of us have phones with push-buttons; people still **hang up** at the end of a call, because the earliest instruments had separate earpieces that the user hung on a lever to terminate the call (phones **off the hook** were unable to receive calls). Workers in television still speak of **filming** an item and of **footage**, although the technology is now almost entirely electronic. It has been many years since **penknives** were last used to trim the points of goose quills; actors still find themselves in the **limelight**, though that type of high-intensity spotlight is long since defunct.

Another type of shift results in a word created with one meaning taking on a figurative sense which then usurps the original: **hotchpotch**, **gallimaufry**, and **balderdash** were once cookery terms; **bombastic** is from a fabric called bombast and **russet** was originally likewise a type of cloth, not a colour; **harbinger** was at first a man sent ahead of a travelling party to organize lodgings; **hazard** started out as a fiendishly complicated dice game; the aircraft or yacht **cockpit** commemorates a cruel sport; **galoshes** were once clogs; a **bugle** was anciently a wild ox, whose horn became a precursor to the musical instrument; **paraphernalia** started out as meaning the personal property of a married woman; and **scuttlebutt** is from the water cask in a ship, around which sailors might gossip.

Too many words have changed their meanings for this to be surprising: an **aftermath** was formerly the new grass growing after mowing or harvest; an **apology** was once a defence against an accusation; a **banquet** was originally a dessert, not a full-scale meal; the earliest sense of **penthouse** was an open-sided shed attached to the side of a building; a **buxom** person was obedient and pliable, and by no means always female; a **chaperone** was in medieval times a cap; to **garble** was to remove the rubbish from spices; in medieval times a **lavatory** was a basin in which to wash onself; the first **muggers**, in the eighteenth century, were hawkers of earthenware; **nice** began its life describing somebody foolish or wanton; **awful** used to be applied to something that inspired awe or was sublime or majestic; a **pittance** was a pious bequest to a medieval religious house to provide extra food and wine at festivals; **snobs** were originally shoe-menders; a **tippler** was a tavern-keeper, only later one who consumed the product of the house; and **bully** started life as an endearment.

But these shifts in terminology are minor compared with the immense list of words that have gone from our everyday vocabularies because the things they refer to are no longer part of our lives. To take a few recent and obvious examples, the change to decimal currency in Britain in 1971 meant that **shilling**, **sixpence**, **half-crown** and several other words became obsolete along with the coins they identified. When we went over to *Value Added Tax (VAT)* in 1973, **purchase tax** became a term only of historical interest. Now that we buy and sell produce in metric quantities, weights and measures like **pounds**, **yards** and **gallons** are hardly understood by younger people; equally obsolescent are degrees **Fahrenheit**, long since officially replaced by *Celsius* (though some of us oldsters recall that the latter was once commonly called **Centigrade** and often translate °C into that).

Changes in male fashion mean that **Oxford bags**, **flares**, **drain-pipe trousers**, and **loon pants** are no longer with us; changes in feminine attire have rendered old-fashioned any reference to **liberty bodices**, **corsets**, **whalebone stays**, **roll-ons**, and **suspenders**, some of them puzzling or even humorous to the young. Changes to the legal and social status of women have rendered obsolete such terms as **career girl** or **girl Friday**. As our homes become fitted as standard with what we regard as the essentials of living, we no longer need to refer to **modern conveniences**, the **all mod cons** of one-time estate-agent speak. Some terms were strictly temporary, such as the **squarial** receiving antenna of the then British Satellite Broadcasting consortium in the late 1980s, or the **millennium bug** that was wrongly feared would bring technology to a halt on 1 January 2000.

This book is an informal investigation of many of these vanishing words. Of course, few of them have completely gone: anyone who is well-read or who has an interest in times past will know many of them, specialists in the history of ideas or material culture many more. Because some continue to appear in films, television programmes, and books with historical settings, you'll find them in larger dictionaries still.

Even though slang has largely been excluded, the field is vast, potentially covering the history of English since its earliest days 1500 years ago, as well as a myriad of subject areas. All human life might be here, were my industry infinite and my publisher's pocket bottomless, though you wouldn't be able to lift the resulting volume. In self-defence, and with due thought to the attention span, even the sanity, of my readers, I have chosen some fragments from this immense canvas to comment on.

Acknowledgements

My particular thanks go to all those at Oxford University Press who have nursed this book through to publication: Judy Pearsall, who suggested the idea, and my editors, Rachel De Wachter and Ben Harris, who helped create its form and gave much good advice, some of which I've even followed. My thanks also go to Mary Wood and Julane Marx, who read the draft text and made many helpful suggestions. For many recent terms, I'm grateful to subscribers to my online newsletter *World Wide Words*, who have helpfully provided me with lists of words that have disappeared or become obsolescent within their lifetimes. My thanks to them all, too many to mention individually. And a special word of thanks, as always, goes to my wife, for trying her best to keep me sane while I was struggling with a chaotic conglomeration of antique vocabulary.

It's impossible to give anything like a comprehensive list of sources of information, since research has ranged so widely over printed works and online sources. The electronic edition of the *Oxford English Dictionary* has been a vital resource, as have other Oxford publications, such as the *Dictionary of National Biography* and the *Grove Dictionary of Music*. Special thanks must go to the volunteers of Project Gutenberg, whose very many freely available complete texts have been an important aid to finding illustrative quotations, as well as to the thousands of institutions and individuals who have created websites to record and communicate their skills, knowledge, and enthusiasms.

PART 1

Food
& Drink

Of messes in pots

MEDIEVAL COOKERY could at its best be as sophisticated in its own way as ours is today, but for ordinary people it consisted of variations on the theme of putting ingredients in a pot of water and boiling them.

Robert Heinlein's novel *Methuselah's Children* includes the line,

> Ford was certain of only one thing: he did not intend to … sell humanity's birthright for a mess of pottage.

Those who know the Bible will recognize the allusion to the story of Esau in Chapter 25 of Genesis, who did exactly that. The phrase *mess of pottage* isn't itself in the 1611 King James Bible, but is in the 1560 Geneva Bible. It's still a common expression, meaning something of little value, though most people who use it would be hard pressed to define either **pottage** or **mess**.

The latter is an obsolete term for a serving of food (it's from Latin *missum*, something put on the table), from which the military *mess* gets its name. *Pottage* comes from French *potage*, a word that may still be found on the menus of posh English restaurants, which meant something put into a pot, hence a stew (in modern French, *potage* means 'soup', a shift similar to one in English that we'll come to in a moment). Jacob actually gave Esau a serving of a stew made from lentils.

The word is obsolete now, but pottages were important in medieval cookery—bread, ale, and pottage were the staples for much of the population. For ordinary people pottages were often no more than oatmeal, boiled vegetables or stewed roots, as in the famous **pease pottage** that many of us remember from the children's rhyme:

> Pease pottage hot, Pease pottage cold,
> Pease pottage in a pot nine days old.

(*Pease*, from Old English *pise*, peas, is the original form, usually plural, that led to *pea* being mistakenly created as the singular.) So totally has *pottage* gone out of use that the rhyme often appears as 'Pease porridge hot...', though as we shall see that's not an unreasonable alteration.

Gravy and **blancmange** were two pottages with names we can still recognize. The former wasn't then the juices of meat we mean by it today—it didn't take on that sense until Elizabethan times—but a more ornate sweet and spicy sauce of ground almonds and broth, seasoned with sugar and ginger, into which were placed small pieces of oysters, eels, rabbit, or chicken. Its name is probably a misreading by scribes of Old French *grané*, a grain of spice. **Blancmange** (originally *blancmanger*, from Old French *blanc mangier*, white food) wasn't a dessert but a mild meat dish without any strong spices in it, containing chicken, rice, almonds, sugar, eggs, and cream. Leave out the meat and you're halfway to our modern version, which became a sweet jelly in the eighteenth century.

The names of most ancient pottages are now unfamiliar, such as **porray**. Strictly speaking, this should have been made from leeks, because the name is from the Latin *purrum*, meaning that vegetable, but the word got confused with the French *purée* and so became a general word for all sorts of thick broths. **White porray** was mainly leeks, but **green porray** (also called **joute**, from the Old French word for a pot-herb or vegetable) was a varied and variable confection of green leaves according to season or what could be taken from the fields or hedgerows, such as beet leaves (a favourite) or **coleworts**. This was a general name for any sort of brassica, which weren't as differentiated as they are now; *cole* is Old English, from Latin *caulis*, cabbage, the origin of our modern *kale*; *wort* was a general name for a useful plant. Other less familiar native English plants might be included, such as docks, borage, or bugloss, possibly with parsley, thyme, mint, or sorrel added to flavour it.

Frumenty (Old French *frumentee* from Latin *frumentum*, corn) in medieval times was often a dish for poor people, being hulled wheat boiled in milk, perhaps with egg yolks beaten in to thicken and colour it (rye or barley were at times substituted for wheat). Better-off households might add almonds, cream, currants, and sugar to enhance the flavour and might serve it with venison; by the eighteenth century it had become a sweet dish served as dessert. It was alcohol-fuelled frumenty, though in the dialect form **furmity**, that led Michael Henchard to sell his wife and child at the village fair in Thomas Hardy's *The Mayor of Casterbridge*.

Grand houses, with better resources and skilled cooks, could ring the changes on a lot of different pottages. They used a variety of sauces that supplied most of the flavour, as well as many of their names, which had usually been brought over from French. **Mortrews** or **mortress** (Old French *morterel* or *morteruel*, a kind of milk soup) was based on milk and bread, with various pounded-up meats added to it, such as chicken or pork. **Blanc dessore** (from Old French; corrupted later to the meaningless English **blank desire**) was similar, sometimes served side by side with **mawmenny** or **malmeny**, essentially chicken with almonds and wine (the origins of these names is obscure). **Egerdouce** was a sweet and sour pottage that included a sauce of raisins, currants, and honey for the sweet flavour and vinegar for the sour (the name is from French *aigre-doux*, sour-sweet, but was Anglicized in various ways, including *eager-dulce* and even *egg-douce*, though it had no eggs in it).

Charlet (from an Old French name for a type of pot) was usually boiled shredded pork mixed with eggs, milk, and saffron seasoning, not so different from **jussell** or **jusshell** (Old French *jussel*, a juice or broth), which was a broth of various meats with eggs, breadcrumbs, and saffron. Yet another pottage was **bukkenade**; the first English cookery book, *The Forme of Cury* (*cury* then meant cookery, from Old French *queurie*), compiled by Richard II's master cooks about 1390, said this was made from chicken, rabbit, veal, or other meat, stewed with almonds, currants, sugar, onions, and salt, thickened if necessary with flour and again coloured with saffron.

Many later recipes confirm that the type of meat in these recipes wasn't important, since the sauce created the flavour. The key feature of **civey** was onions (its name isn't French, but Old English, from *cipe*, a type of onion, from which we get *chive*). **Cullis** (ultimately from Latin *colare*, to strain or sieve) is recorded from the early fifteenth century. It was often made with chicken—though other meats or sometimes fish could replace it—which was boiled and strained to make a thick broth considered good for invalids. In the eighteenth century one variety became known as **beef tea**. **Amidon** was a thickener of wheat starch, a kind of cornflour; Roman writers such as Pliny and Cato knew it as *amulum*; it's from Latin *amylum*, starch.

In the sixteenth century the term **hasty pudding** began to be applied to an ancient dish of flour boiled in water to a thick consistency, with milk or beer added afterwards; the name comes from the speed with which it could be prepared, not quite up to today's instant mixes, but quick enough. This was as much a **porridge** as a pottage, and indeed the word *porridge* evolved from *pottage*, though the first porridges often contained vegetables, herbs, or meat and the word was applied specifically to a salted or sweetened oatmeal dish only in the 1640s. Another name for the dish in Scotland and Northern England was **crowdie**, a word of unknown origin which seems unconnected with the much more recent term for a type of Scottish cottage cheese often served with cream.

A similar dish was **flummery** (from Welsh *llymru*; perhaps related to *llymrig*, soft or slippery), first mentioned by Gervase Markham in his *English Housewife* of 1623. He called it 'an excellent dish' of 'wholesomeness and rare goodness'; it was made by steeping wheatmeal or oatmeal in water, then straining and boiling it until it was 'a thick and stiff jelly'; it was served with honey, wine, beer, or milk. Later that century the name was applied to a light, sweet dish made with eggs and flour, whose name was borrowed in the next century to describe empty compliments or nonsense; in 1749 Lady Luxborough wrote in a letter,

> This word flummery, you must know, Sir, means at
> London, flattery, and compliment.

As the centuries passed, pottages went out of favour and their components were separately developed, with the meat element being served instead as **fricassées**, **hashes**, **ragouts**, and similar dishes, and the sauces becoming distinct culinary items. All three words are French: *fricassée* from *fricasser*, to cut up and cook in sauce; *hash* via *hacher*, to cut up, from *hache*, hatchet; and *ragout* from *ragoûter*, to revive the taste of a dish.

The thin broth derived from stewing meat also began to be served as a separate course, for which another French word, *soupe*, was borrowed; in French this meant broth poured on slices of bread, a thing commonly done in earlier centuries with pottages, and for which the closely related English **sop** was used. **Soup** only came into the English language in the middle of the seventeenth century; one of its earliest users was the ever-fashionable Samuel Pepys, who recorded in his *Diary* on 15 March 1668:

> W. Hewer and I did walk to the Cocke, at the end
> of Suffolke Streete ... and dined very handsome,
> with a good soup, and a pullet, for 4s. 6d. the
> whole.

Pepys was very fond of his food. Some of the meals described in his diary might cause indigestion today just from reading about them, as here from 4 April 1663:

> We had a fricasee of rabbits and chickens, a leg of mutton boiled, three carps in a dish, a great dish of a side of lamb, a dish of roasted pigeons, a dish of four lobsters, three tarts, a lamprey pie (a most rare pie), a dish of anchovies, good wine of several sorts, and all things mighty noble and to my great content.

Lampreys (from Latin *lambere*, to lick + *petra*, stone, because the lamprey attaches itself to rocks by its mouth) are a native eel-like freshwater fish, notorious for supposedly having caused the death of Henry I (though the *Dictionary of National Biography* says firmly, "The legend that Henry died of 'a surfeit of lampreys' has no basis in the historical record. It was not that he ate too many lampreys, but that his physician had advised him not to eat any at all"); in **lamprey pie** they were baked in butter, drained, and then sealed under more butter so they would keep; Pepys's pie almost certainly came up from Gloucester and contained the famous Severn lampreys. Pepys also mentions **hog's pudding**, an early type of sausage that today is regarded as a traditional Cornish dish; in his time the entrails of a hog were stuffed with a mixture either of oatmeal, suet, and tripe, or of flour, currants, and spices.

In July 1663 Pepys recorded eating **umbles**:

> Mrs. Turner came in, and did bring us an umble pie
> hot out of her oven, extraordinary good.

Umbles were originally *numbles* (that first letter was especially variable, since the original was Latin *lumbulus*, the diminutive of *lumbus*, loin), which were the innards of the deer—the liver, heart, entrails, and other third-class bits. It was common practice in medieval times after a hunt to serve **umble pie** made from these parts of the animal to the servants who had taken part. In the nineteenth century, in the phrase **eating humble pie**, and with a nod to its lowly origins, it was created as a punning term for the state of being deeply apologetic. In Pepys's day, it clearly had a higher status, since he records serving it to his boss Sir William Batten, Surveyor of the Navy; Pepys is often rude about Batten in his diary, but would hardly feed him low-class rubbish.

Pepys doesn't record **salmagundi** because the name is first recorded shortly after he stopped writing his diary for fear of his eyesight failing. It has been known by many names, including **salladmagundy** and **Solomon Gundy** (it can be traced back to the French *salmigondis*, but there the etymological trail goes cold, though theories abound). Like its name it was a rather variable dish. Elizabeth Moxon, in her *English Housewife* in 1764, describes it as a Lenten dish and instructs the cook to take "herrings, a quarter of a pound of anchovies, a large apple, a little onion ... or shalot, and a little lemon-peel" and shred them all together. Other recipes suggested eggs, chicken, almonds, grapes, and raisins as ingredients. This highly variable mix led *salmagundi* later to take on the sense of a mixture or miscellany. Solomon Gundy was also sometimes known as **Solomon Grundy**, which may explain the nursery rhyme about 'Solomon Grundy, born on a Monday ...' and the name of **Mrs Grundy**, the personification of social conformity and disapproval, whose name first appears in Thomas Morton's play *Speed the Plough* in 1798.

Other terms for confused concoctions also come from cookery. A **hotchpotch** or **hodgepodge** was in the fifteenth century a meat broth or pottage that contained a lot of ingredients (its first form was *hotchpot*, from the French word that contained the verb *hocher*, to shake, suggesting ingredients mixed up in a pot; later versions are popular misunderstandings that turned the term into a rhyming couplet). Another, from the next century, is **gallimaufry** (French *galimafrée*, a word of unknown origin), a hash made up of odds and ends of leftovers. In the seventeenth century, **balderdash**, now meaning nonsense, was an unappetizing mixture of incompatible drinks, such as beer and milk or beer and wine; despite lots of theories, nobody knows where this one comes from, though some suspect *balductum* (*see page* 62).

Sugar and spice and all things nice

MANY FOODS of the medieval period were bland and samey and needed to be enlivened with exotic ingredients, if you could afford them.

In those times almost every food came highly spiced. This was partly to hide the taste of meat that was of poor quality or had been preserved by salting—though not to disguise the off-flavours of rotten meat, as is often claimed—but mainly because people in the period after the Norman Conquest just liked highly seasoned food if they could get it and could afford it.

Many of their spices are still widely used today: **pepper**, **mace**, **cloves**, **mustard**, **cinnamon**, **ginger**, **saffron**, **nutmeg**. Another was **sugar**, which we don't think of in the same way, but which was an expensive and exotic condiment when it first appeared in the eleventh century; it was then thought to be as much medicinal as culinary and only when it became widely available in later centuries did it replace the traditional sweetener, honey.

Other spices have gone out of use or are narrowly known to enthusiasts or specialists. Take **zedoary** from Bengal, whose name was often corrupted in English to **setwall**. It's a close relative of turmeric, popular in medieval Europe but later replaced by ginger. It was sometimes added to wine as a flavouring, but nobody much below the rank of king could afford to do so, it being rare and expensive (Henry III is one who is recorded as having some of his Christmas wine flavoured with it in 1244). It was confused with **zerumbet**, another Indian spice, a kind of wild ginger.

Like most spices and herbs, both zedoary and zerumbet (their names were originally from Persian, respectively *zidwār* and *zerunbād*) were used in medicine; Nicholas Culpeper knew they were different, but said in *The Complete Herbal* in 1653 that their effects were the same:

> They are both hot and dry in the second degree, expel wind, resist poison, stop fluxes, and the menses, stay vomiting, help the cholic, and kill worms.

A third ginger-like spice used in cooking was variously called **galingale**, **galangal**, or **galanga** (names that come via Arabic from the Chinese *Ko-liang-kiang*, 'the mild ginger from Ko'). Culpeper recommended it, among other purposes, to treat 'moisture of the stomach':

> Take a drachm of Galanga, in powder, every
> morning in a draught of that Wine you like best.

Henry III had more of his Christmas wine in 1244 flavoured with another spice: **cubeb** (from Arabic *kabābah*), a relative of black pepper, though more bitter. It was used in cookery and it was prescribed for urinary problems as well. Cubeb went out of favour in the seventeenth century, but the oil came back into use in the British Army in Java and India in the nineteenth century to treat gonorrhoea, confirming that the herbalists of an earlier century were on the right track. Americans would once have known of **cubeb cigarettes**, smoked like the mentholated type, and available from the late nineteenth century well into the twentieth. An advertisement from 1913 for Requa's Cubeb Cigarettes claimed they were

> a remedy for catarrh, cold in the head, asthma,
> hay fever, foul breath, etc. Contains no tobacco.

Another favourite medieval spice was **grains of paradise**, a wonderful name for a type of pepper, reflecting the old idea that the earthly paradise was scented with spices. It came from the Guinea coast of West Africa and other names for it were **Guinea pepper** and **Guinea grains**. It was used both in cookery and in

medicine, like all spices, but it was an especial favourite with
which to flavour wines, including *hippocras* (*see page 34*).

Some medieval and Renaissance spices were compounded into
mixtures that long remained popular, though what went into
them has been debated for centuries and nobody is sure even
now. Since they were usually home-made, no doubt they varied
from cook to cook and depended on what was available. **Poudre
douce** (mild spice), possibly the same thing as **poudre blanch**
(white spice), seems to have been a mixture of sugar, ginger, and
cinnamon. In 1460 John Russell wrote in the *Book of Nurture* (in
modernized spelling):

> After supper, roasted apples, pears, blanch
> powder, your stomach for to ease.

Sir Thomas Cogan wrote in 1612 that it was very good

> to strew upon roasted apples, quinces or
> wardens, or to sauce a hen

(**wardens** were a type of pear good for baking). **Poudre fort**
(strong spice) was employed like our modern curry powder
or five-spice powder and contained the hotter spices, such as
various peppers, cloves, nutmeg, mace, cinnamon, ginger, and
perhaps grains of paradise; it was eclipsed by curry powders
brought back from India by the Portuguese in the early sixteenth
century. Yet another mixture from the seventeenth century and

afterwards was called **kitchen pepper**, still known to some extent. An 1840 recipe by Eliza Leslie said it was

> a mixture, in equal quantities, of black or white pepper, allspice, cinnamon, cloves, ginger and nutmeg.

As well as spices, medieval cookery was very strong on sauces, which were often so powerful that they overwhelmed the meat element of the dish.

A common medieval sauce was called **camelyn** or **cameline**, the latter being confusingly also the name of a type of cloth supposedly made from camel's hair; *camelyn* may be from *canel*, an old name for cinnamon. It consisted of white bread, vinegar, cinnamon, ginger, and a little sugar, often the partly-refined dark sugar that contained a lot of molasses. The *Forme of Cury* suggested adding raisins, cloves, and nuts. It was served with various roast birds, such as **heronsewe** (a young heron, from Old French *heroncel*), egret, crane, bittern, shoveller, plover, and bustard.

Botargo was the sixteenth-century English name of a relish made from the roe of the grey mullet (sometimes the tunny) that was known to the Greeks of classical times and all around the Mediterranean. Its name is Arabic—*butarkhah*, meaning preserved mullet-roe, though the English relish was actually imported from Italy. It looked like wax-coated dark-brown bananas that were then sliced thin. **Peverade** (from Norman French *peivre*, pepper) was a pepper sauce which the *Forme of Cury* said should be served with venison or veal, though later writers suggested it went best with brawn. **Chawdron** (from French *chaudière*, a pot, the source also of *chowder*) was a spice of the chopped entrails of some animal with vinegar and spices; in medieval times it was often made from the innards of swans in particular and served with that dish. Shakespeare wove the word into a bit of wordplay chanted by the witches in *Macbeth*:

> Make the gruel thick and slab.
> Add thereto a tiger's chawdron,
> For the ingredients of our cauldron.

Some dishes had much simpler sauces, perhaps just vinegar or **verjuice**. The latter (literally "green juice" in French) was the juice of green or unripe grapes, or of crab apples or other sour fruit. It went with various fish or light meat dishes, such as bream, sole, veal, or chicken, and continued to appear in recipes until the nineteenth century (modern instructions to "add a dash of lemon juice" are almost a direct replacement). Another condiment of similar function was **alegar** (English *ale* + French *aigre*, sour), which was similar in function and if anything more important, later replacing verjuice in pickles and sauces; it was made from the wort of unhopped ale, and we know it today better as malt vinegar.

A **lear** (the spelling varied down the centuries, with **layour**, **leir**, and **leer** also being recorded) was a thickening agent for sauces, or a sauce that had been thickened. Literally it tied the ingredients together, since the name comes via French from the same Latin source as *ligature*. In *The Compleat Cook* in 1655, Nathaniel Brook gave a recipe for sheep feet:

> When you think they are fryed almost enough,
> have a lear made for them with the yolks of two or
> three Eggs, some Gravy of Mutton, a little
> Nutmegg, and juyce of a Lemon wrung therein,
> and put this lear to the Sheeps feet as they fry in
> the Pan.

In *The Art of Cookery Made Plain and Easy* in 1805, Mrs. Glasse recommended cooking shrimps in "a stewpan with a spoonful of fish-lear, or anchovy-liquor".

Skilligalee and boiled babies

I F YOU FEEL that some of the foods in the previous chapter, even spiced and sauced, were a bit boring or unhealthy, you may be shocked by their nautical equivalents.

Having come late in life to the seafaring novels of Patrick O'Brian, I've been privileged to read the whole lot through from start to finish in short order, several times. What must strike any reader is how important food is to Captain Aubrey and his officers and men and how awful most of it is.

One such dish was given the especially unappetizing name of **boiled baby**, or **drowned baby**. Here it appears in *Clarissa Oakes*:

> As we could not put into Fiji for hogs, contrary winds obliging us to bear away for Tonga, she may be a mother before ever she sits down to the

> banquet, unless they will be content with a plain
> sea-pie accompanied by dog's-body and followed
> by boiled baby.

Basically, boiled baby was a suet pudding, the suet being garnished with nutmeg, raisins, and cinnamon and boiled in a sausage-shaped bag of muslin, which did give it the rather unfortunate appearance of a deceased infant in swaddling clothes.

Of those other dishes mentioned in the quotation, we now think of a **dog's body** or **dogsbody** as a person who gets all the boring and menial jobs to do. But long before that it was another name for **pease pudding**, essentially dried peas boiled in a pudding cloth with some flour, salt, and pepper. One can only sympathize with the sailors in another sea yarn about the same period, *Hornblower in the West Indies* by C S Forester:

> Salt beef and pease pudding under a noonday sun
> in the tropics—who could have any appetite for
> that, especially with the excitement of watching
> for a wind?

When cold, you could cut dog's body into slices and eat it on the go. Why sailors should have called it that is hard to see (though if they could call a suet pudding boiled baby they were capable of almost anything in the nomenclatural line). And it's unclear whether there's any link between the food sense and the modern menial one.

The first-named dish in the quotation might seem obvious enough. Surely a **sea-pie** contained fish? Actually, no. It was called that because it was a dish made at sea, not because it contained any fruits of the ocean. The key aspect of a sea-pie was explained to Stephen Maturin by Captain Aubrey in *The Far Side of the World*:

> "Pies at sea," he said, "are made on nautical lines, of course. They are quite unlike pies by land. First you lay down a stratum of pastry, then a layer of meat, then a layer of pastry, then another layer of meat, and so on, according to the number of decks required."

Smaller ships with limited resources had to make do with what they could manage. Often these came down to "throw what's available into a pot and boil it". Stephen Maturin's little daughter Brigid discovers this when she sails in the small ship called the *Ringle* (recounted in *The Commodore*):

> Eventually, with darkness gathering, she was brought aft and below, dried, put down in front of a bowl of lobscouse (the *Ringle*'s only dish, apart from skillygalee or burgoo) and desired to "tuck in, mate, tuck in like a good 'un."

Lobscouse was a one-pot stew, a more substantial one than either of the available alternatives of skilligalee or burgoo, since it consisted of meat, ship's biscuit, and vegetables such as onions or leeks. Its name is a mystery: there are related words in Norwegian, Danish, Dutch, and German, though whether we borrowed it from them or they from us is unclear. However, we do know that sailors also called it **scouse** and that it lent its name to the people of Liverpool, *Scousers*, because it was a port city in which they ate a lot of scouse. A closely related dish was called **loblolly**, a rural dish whose name may come from the dialect *lob*, to boil. Both lobscouse and loblolly had a good reputation, on shore as well as at sea, as filling foods. But the latter was often viewed as a medical remedy, which is why ships had *loblolly boys* as lowly assistants to the ship's surgeon, because one of their jobs was to feed the patients.

The name of **skilligalee** (or **skillygalee**) seems to have originally been Irish, though fancifully extended, and then abbreviated again to **skilly**, often used as a dismissive term for any insipid beverage. It was a thin oatmeal gruel or porridge. In 1820 James Hardy Vaux disparaged it in his *Memoirs*:

> Tolerable flour, of which the cook composed a
> certain food for breakfast, known among sailors
> by the name of skilligolee, being in plain English,
> paste.

(Other writers of that century and the next also compared skilly to bill-sticker's paste, presumably because of its consistency rather than its taste.) If you were extremely lucky, sugar and butter were added, though common sailors were rarely so fortunate. Nor were workhouse inmates, for whom this was standard fare.

Burgoo was similar (its name came into English via the Turkish *bulgur* from a Persian word for wheat that has been cooked, dried, and crushed). In the US, burgoo was a substantial frontier dish of wild game, such as venison, squirrel, rabbit, opossum, raccoon, quail, or wild turkey, slow-cooked outdoors in big iron pots; later, chicken, pork, and vegetables were among the ingredients. It's linked especially with Kentucky, where it has been traditionally served at a barbecue during the weekend of the Kentucky Derby, though in 2003 the *Kentucky Post* lamented that "Burgoo's heyday is gone." On board ships during the Napoleonic Wars, it was thin fare, which was described in *The Far Side of the World* as "a kind of liquid porridge". Its main advantage was that it was served hot.

Figgy-dowdy or **figgy-dowdie** was a type of plum pudding. A graphic account of how to make it is included in *Post Captain*:

> Canning eyed the pale, amorphous, gleaming, slightly translucent mass and asked how it was made; he did not think he had ever seen anything quite like it. "We take ship's biscuit, put it in a stout canvas bag -" said Jack. "Pound it with a marlin-spike for half an hour -" said Pullings. "Add bits of pork fat, plums, figs, rum, currants,"

> said Parker. "Send it to the galley, and serve it up
> with bosun's grog," said Macdonald.

Do not assume by the mention of figs that that's where the name comes from. *Figgy* here is from an old West Country sense of *fig*, meaning a raisin or currant (that's not the oddest sense of the word: at one time in the East and West Indies a fig was a banana). *Dowdy* here is presumably the dialect sense of something dull-coloured.

Duff was just a flour pudding boiled or steamed in a cloth bag (the word is a northern form of *dough*); **plum-duff** or **currant duff** was duff with raisins or currants in it, the former having that name because by *plums* sailors often meant dried fruit. In *Mr Midshipman Hornblower* the young Hornblower is entranced by dinner at the Dalrymples:

> The final dishes, the meringues and macaroons,
> the custards and the fruits, were ecstasy for a
> young man whose last pudding had been currant
> duff last Sunday.

Ship's biscuit or **hard-tack** was a coarse biscuit of flour and water, baked and dried so that it was rock hard but would keep for a year on board ship. **Soft-tack** was everyday bread—the brown sort, considered inferior to white—which was available only in port or shortly after setting to sea. In both cases, *tack* is an old term for a foodstuff, of obscure origin, though it might be a shortened form of *tackle*, with the idea behind it that food was considered part of the equipment of the ship. Sailors also used the soldiers' name for the brown bread of their rations, **soft tommy**. (*Tommy* is from *Tom*, as a personification of food; though it might seem to be the origin of **Tommy** as an old nickname for the British soldier, that's instead from *Thomas Atkins*, a fake name that appeared in specimen completed official forms in the British army during the nineteenth century.)

Boiling up the unappetizing salt pork and salt beef resulted in a mass of semi-liquid fat. This was called **slush**, stored in a **slush-tub**. Some was used to grease tackle blocks, running rigging, and the like. Selling what remained was often a perk of the ship's cook, some to members of the crew for frying biscuit or the occasional fresh-caught fish, the rest to tallow chandlers in port for making candles. The proceeds were sometimes supposed instead to be paid into a **slush fund** to pay for small luxuries for the crew. In the US of the 1870s that term began to be used for an unofficial source of money to be used for what the *Glasgow Herald* in 1924 referred to as "illicit commission, bribery, corruption, and graft".

A couple of favourites of Patrick O'Brian's characters with which to leave the books for now. *The Nutmeg of Consolation* records that Stephen Maturin "was fond of a pair of cold crubeens". **Crubeen** is an Anglo-Irish word for a pig's trotter, from the Irish *crúibín* which is derived from *crúb*, a claw or hoof.

A favourite of Captain Aubrey was a kind of dessert called a **floating island**, which was a meringue, or perhaps several, floated on a sea of custard.

One concoction not mentioned in Patrick O'Brian's books is **geograffy**, a word of unknown origin, though Captain Frederick Marryat said it was a corruption of *geography*. He gives a recipe in his novel *Newton Forster* of 1832:

> Take a tin-pot, go to the scuttle-butt (having obtained permission from the quarter-deck), and draw off about half a pint of very offensive smelling water. To this add a gill of vinegar and a ship's biscuit broke up into small pieces. Stir it well up with the fore-finger; and then with the fore-finger and thumb you may pull out the pieces of biscuit, and eat them as fast as you please, drinking the liquor to wash all down.

You can see why it was so common for sailors to suffer deficiency diseases such as scurvy on long sea journeys. Today such a diet would be regarded as cruel and unusual punishment rather than just unhealthy.

Fruits of grain and grape

NO FOOD, whether afloat or on dry land, in modern time or ancient, was complete without something alcoholic to accompany it.

Mead, the drink of lords and thanes that was celebrated in *Beowulf* and the *Mabinogion*, is still well known though not much drunk. We can trace its name back to an Indo-European root that turns up in Sanskrit *madhu*, a sweet drink of honey, and in Greek *methu*, wine. By the end of the Plantagenet period mead had rather gone out of fashion in favour of spiced wines. The Welsh had a variant which they called **metheglin** (from the Welsh *meddyglyn*, physician, because it was said to be medicinal, which sounds like a good excuse for a hearty quaff or two), which was mead spiced with cloves, ginger, rosemary, hyssop, and thyme. **Hydromel** (a mixture of honey and water, from Greek *hudro-*, water + *meli*, honey) was either another name for mead or a weaker variety of that drink. Much later, around the beginning of the nineteenth century, **morat** (Latin *mōrus*, mulberry) appeared, which was mead flavoured with mulberries.

Ale was the traditional everyday drink made from fermented barley, wheat, or oats. Before the Norman Conquest *beer* and *ale* referred to the same drink, but after hops were introduced around 1525 **beer** began to be used for the hopped type; today the way brewers use the two words is rather complicated. Water was universally considered to be unpotable or even dangerous. In 1621, Robert Burton wrote in the *Anatomy of Melancholy* that waters from ponds and other sources were

> unfit to make drink of, to dress meat with, or to be used about men inwardly or outwardly. They are good for many domestic uses, to wash horses, water cattle, etc, or in time of necessity, but not otherwise.

So ale was drunk at every opportunity, often enough that it gave its name to special occasions: **bride-ale** (a wedding feast), **dirge-ale** (an ale-drinking at a funeral), **hocking-ale** (the festival of Hocktide, the second Monday and Tuesday after Easter, a name on whose history gallons of ink have been expended with no very useful result), **lamb-ale** (an annual feast at lambing time), **leet-ale** (the customary drinking after the annual court-leet had met before the lord of the manor, where *leet* is an old Anglo-Norman word we don't know much about), and many more.

Unhopped ale quickly went off. It was common to add herbs and spices to it to improve its taste and help it keep. **Alehoof**, **hayhove**, **tunhoof**, and **hove** (all derived from Old English *hófe*) were names for ground ivy, a frequent flavouring. Another was **alecost** (from Latin *costus*, the name of a quite different aromatic plant from Kashmir with a similar smell), or **costmary** (because it was often associated with Mary, mother of Jesus) or just **cost**; this was a native of the Near East, allied to the tansy, which was widely cultivated in Europe in late medieval times; Culpeper called it **balsam herb** and said it was in almost every English garden. **Purl** (origin unknown) or **wormwood ale** was flavoured with an infusion of wormwood or other bitter herbs. If the infusion was in wine instead, it was called **purl-royal**. It stayed a favourite with Londoners into the nineteenth century, though by this time purl was usually instead a mixture of ale and gin, also called **dog's nose**. Charles Dickens mentions it several times, as here in *Barnaby Rudge*:

> It was now broad day, but the morning being cold, a group of them were gathered round a fire in a public-house, drinking hot purl, and smoking pipes, and planning new schemes for to-morrow.

Dickens also mentions **flip**, beer and spirits sweetened with sugar and heated with a hot iron.

A mixture of honey and ale fermented together and spiced with pepper was called **bragget**, **braggot**, or **bragwort**, whose name derives from an ancient Celtic word for a kind of grain. By the fifteenth century bragget had become a more complex drink, being flavoured with cinnamon, pepper, cloves, ginger, and galingale. In the *Canterbury Tales*, Geoffrey Chaucer wrote, "Her mouth was sweet as braket or as methe", that is, as sweet as either bragget or mead. The fourth Sunday in Lent was once called **Bragget Sunday** or **Braggot Sunday** through a custom of drinking bragget on that day.

In the fourteenth century, there's mention of **piriwhit**, a mixture of cheap ale and perry that was sold to poorer people (*perry* is the pear equivalent of cider). Our knowledge of it comes largely from the contemporary poem *Piers Plowman* by William Langland, which speaks of "penny ale and piriwhit" and also of another low-quality type called **pudding ale**; this was perhaps so called because it was thickened, but more probably because it was sold before the yeast dregs had had time to settle out. **Aleberry**, however, was deliberately thickened, being ale or beer boiled with spices, sugar, and bread, often taken as a warming early-morning drink or as invalid food. **Buttered ale** was similar, ale boiled with butter, sugar, and cinnamon and thickened with beaten eggs. From the end of the sixteenth century, there's mention of **lambswool**, hot ale mixed with the pulp of roasted apples and the inevitable sugar and spices. **China-ale** in the seventeenth century was flavoured with **China-root**, which was rather like sarsaparilla and imbued with medicinal properties. Pepys records drinking it at a China-ale house in 1662 and later mentions **horse-radish ale**. **White ale** was once well known around Kingsbridge in South Devon; beer was brewed with flour, milk, and eggs, which gave it a grey-white colour. And around 1700, long before **hot-pot** was a dish, it was a hot drink of ale and spirits, or ale sweetened and spiced.

By the time of the first Queen Elizabeth some very strong ales and beers were being brewed, such as **huffcap**, a drink that figuratively *huffs*, or raises, the cap, and **doble-doble**, meaning double-double, presumably therefore very strong. The former was also called **hum cap** in the *Dictionary of the Vulgar Tongue* of 1811. In the sixteenth century, a strong, heady ale with a good foaming head might be called **noppy ale** or **nappie ale**, presumably because the head was like the *nap* on a carpet. **Stingo** is another strong ale, whose name is recorded from the seventeenth century and which is especially linked with Yorkshire. A pub called the *Yorkshire Stingo* once stood in Marylebone Road in London; George Shillibeer started the first public bus service in Britain from there on 4 July 1829. Other strong ales were graced with slangy names such as **knock-me-down** and **merry-go-down**.

Adam's ale, of course, was plain water.

Of drinks from grapes, many that were once common have vanished into history as our tastes have changed. With them have gone their names, so that reading older texts can require keeping a dictionary handy to make sense of what the characters are consuming.

Take **malmsey** (from *Monemvasia* in the Peloponnese, corrupted in French to *malvoisie* and further altered during its transfer to English). Famously, the ill-fated Duke of Clarence, brother to Richard III, was said to have been executed by drowning in a butt of malmsey, his favourite tipple. It was a sweet white wine that by the time of toper George's demise was being made in Spain, the Azores, Madeira, and the Canaries as well as in Greece (the sweetest grade of madeira today retains the name). A similar wine from Italy was called **vernage**, an English version of the name of the ancient Tuscan *vernaccia*, which is still made.

Many other strong sweet wines were drunk at around the same time, mostly too rich or "hot" to be drunk with meat meals, but which were served with salads or fruit. **Tyre** was probably named after the place in Syria but it was actually made in Calabria or Sicily. **Rochelle** derives its name from La Rochelle, the seaport in France from which it was exported to Britain. **Rumney** or **romney** (from Romania, a name then used of mainland Greece) was a resinated wine from Greece. **Bastard**, an odd name whose origin is puzzling, was a sweet Spanish wine whose name sometimes attached to any sweetened wine—Shakespeare puts it into the mouth of Prince Hal in *Henry IV*: "Score a Pint of Bastard in the Halfe Moone"; a variety was called **brown bastard**. In *Henry VI*, Shakespeare mentions **charneco**, a popular Portuguese wine of the period whose name is that of a village near Lisbon; so far as I can discover, however, he doesn't include **hollock** (Spanish *aloque*, light red, originally from Arabic), a type of Spanish red wine. **Osey** (a corruption of *vin d'Aussay*, the wine of Alsace) was a sweet French wine. **Alicant** was known from the end of the fifteenth century and stayed popular for 200 years; it was a rough and rather sweet red wine from Alicante in south-east Spain. **Tent** (Spanish *tinto*, dark-coloured) was another Spanish red wine of the period, which stayed popular somewhat longer. One of the oddest names is **Peter-see-me**, the corrupted name of a seventeenth-century sweet white wine made from a Spanish grape variety, still grown, called Pedro Ximenes after the man who introduced it to Spain. In the following century **liatico** was a red wine made in Tuscany and a grape variety of that name is still grown in Crete.

Many people of this and earlier periods right back to Roman times liked their wine spiced, a habit developed to disguise thin or off flavours and the rough taste of most wines, which were drunk young because they didn't keep. The oldest of these in England was **piment** (from Old French, cognate with the medieval Latin *pigmentum* for a spiced drink and later transferred in the form *pimento* to the spice itself) which was a white wine with added honey and spices, usually pepper. Piment was imported into England even before the Norman Conquest and was much imitated.

By Chaucer's time, two of these spicy wines that were especially popular were called **hippocras** and **clary**; he mentions them in the *Canterbury Tales*:

> He drinkith ypocras, clarre, and vernage
> Of spices hote, to encrese his corrage.

Hippocras took its name from the conical bag through which it was strained, which was said to resemble the sleeve of the classical Greek physician Hippocrates, or at least the shape of the sleeves of medieval gowns. It was a red wine, flavoured with ginger, cinnamon, and grains of paradise and sweetened either with honey or, if you could afford it, with sugar. Clary was an even sweeter drink with a lot of extra sugar or honey and with many spices, including pepper and ginger; its name comes from the medieval Latin *claretum*, "that which is clarified", from which we also get the name of the modern red wine *claret*.

The best-known of these old wines is **sack**, because of its connections with Shakespeare's Sir John Falstaff; it was an amber-coloured sweet wine from southern Spain and the Canaries. The name perhaps comes from the French *sec*, meaning "dry" in the sense that all the sugar has been converted into alcohol. It seems that we took over *vin sec* but kept only the second word without worrying about its literal meaning. It was clearly not always sweet enough for the Elizabethan palate, for Sir John speaks several times of "sack and sugar", a sly dig at his extravagance which is lost on us now, sugar no longer being the expensive spice it once was.

He also refers to **sherris sack**, because much of the sack drunk in England came from the southern Spanish province of Jerez, of which *sherris* is a corruption. Even during Shakespeare's lifetime, the word was shortened to **sherry**, perhaps because people mistakenly thought *sherris* was a plural. The modern sherry is a descendant of Falstaff's sack, though shortly after his day it began to be made by the more complicated modern process which includes adding brandy. Because so much of it came into England via the port of Bristol, it was slangily called **Bristol milk**, hence the modern brand called *Bristol Cream*.

Most of the wines that became popular in the seventeenth century and after are with us still, many of them called after the area in which they were created, such as **burgundy**, **chianti**, **moselle**, and **champagne**. **Malaga** was named after the Spanish town from which it was exported; it was also often called **mountain** or **mountain wine** in the eighteenth century, as the grapes were grown in high vineyards. The German wine called **hock** was first called **hockamore**, an English form of *Hochheimer*, from Hochheim on the river Main. **Port** takes its name from Oporto in Portugal. **Vermouth** contained wormwood (*vermout* in French) to flavour it. **Rum** is more mysterious; when it first appeared in Barbados in the seventeenth century it was called **rumbullion**, though nobody seems to know why.

Some wines of this period have gone out of memory, such as **frontiniac**, from Frontignan in France. William Wordsworth mentioned it in the introduction to his *Lyrical Ballads* of 1800 in a complaint about men

> who will converse with us as gravely about a *taste* for Poetry, as they express it, as if it were a thing as indifferent as a taste for rope-dancing, or Frontiniac or Sherry.

Below-stairs life

TO VISIT the kitchen of a big house centuries ago was to enter a world very different to anything we know today. Not only were the cooking methods and equipment different, but the names and duties of the servants who cooked and served the meals were unfamiliar.

In a now forgotten American book of 1886, *The Knights of the White Shield*, Edward Rand had a character reminisce about his daughter:

> She made pies—cooked 'em, I mean—in a brick oven, and she stewed her chickens in pots hung on hooks from a swinging crane in the chimney. And then I gave Jerusha a turn-spit, too, which she put before the fire, and I gave her a tin kitchen.

In those few words are brought together some of the words connected with old kitchens that—like the book and its author—are now just footnotes in history.

The typical arrangement was a chimney breast housing an open fire with small ovens built into the walls. A variety of gadgets helped the cooks to do their job. The most substantial of these was the **spit** for roasting joints of meat in front of the fire—a set of horizontal rods supported in hooks in a pair of uprights sometimes called **cobbards** or **cobirons**. The first part of these names is from *cob* in the sense of a knob (we don't know where this sense of *cob* comes from, though the first examples referred to a chief or leader, perhaps implying a head or top). The spit had to be turned all the time during cooking to heat the meat evenly on all sides. The **turn-spit** (or **turnspit**) of Edward Rand's text was almost certainly a clockwork device, though the first contrivances by that name—in the late sixteenth century—were treadmills containing a small dog who ran unceasingly to turn the spits connected to it.

In older periods, the turning of the spit was done by hand by a boy or some menial servant, a job that you may imagine was both boring and excessively hot. He might likewise have been called a **turnspit**, from about 1600 on, but the medieval name was **turnbroach**, since the earliest spits consisted of pointed wood skewers or metal rods called **broaches** thrust into the meat. By the time Harrison Ainsworth used *turnbroach* in *The Lancashire Witches* in 1849, it was archaic:

> They could see through the wicket a great fire
> blazing and crackling on the green, with a huge

> carcass on an immense spit before it, and a
> couple of turnbroaches basting it.

Broach is the same word as *brooch*, both originally meaning something sharp or pointed; both forms are from the Old French word *broche*, a spit for roasting, based on Latin *brocca*, a spike or pointed instrument (the verb *to broach* meaning to introduce a difficult subject derives figuratively from the same source). In medieval times the turnbroach might have had the name of **hasteler**; this comes via Old French *haste*, a spit, from Latin *hasta*, a spear. *Haslet*, for pork offal pressed into a loaf and cooked, is from the same source, because originally it was a piece of meat for roasting that had been made up from the innards of an animal.

Another type of spit was hung vertically inside the chimney. Sometimes it was called a **dangle-spit** or **jack**; the latter name was taken from a generic name for a male servant (as in *Jack-of-all-work* or *Jack-of-all-trades*), which was also given to anything that did the job of a person. The chimney spit only became practicable when ways were worked out to turn it automatically, since servants couldn't easily get at it. An early type was the **smokejack**, which was turned by the current of air passing up the chimney from the fire below. Samuel Pepys records in his *Diary* visiting a Mr Spong in October 1660:

> After supper we looked over many books, and
> instruments of his, especially his wooden jack in

> his chimney, which goes with the smoke, which
> indeed is very pretty.

The device wasn't especially effective, because it so often became choked with soot and jammed. Later models, as I say, were driven by clockwork; in the nineteenth century, these were known sometimes as **bottlejacks** because of their shape. In that century, a semicircular metal stand, a **roasting screen**, was often placed in front of the roast to help it cook by reflecting heat back; Victorians called a later type with a built-in jack a **hastener** (because it speeded up the roasting process) or a **Dutch oven**, though the latter was strictly a pot with a lid that was heated in the fire by heaping coals around it (it was presumably given that name because the technique was borrowed from the Netherlands). It's the same device that Edward Rand called a **tin kitchen**, though this was a New England term.

Chimney jacks were hung from a horizontal bar sometimes called the **crook-tree**, because it also supported the **crooks** or **pothooks** on which the various cooking pots were suspended. These were often fitted with **trammels**, devices consisting of a series of rings or links that allowed the height of the pot to be altered. The original *trammel* was a type of net made up of three layers, whose name comes from Latin *tres*, three + *macula*, mesh; both this sense and our modern noun and verb that refer to impeding or confining come from the idea of entrapment or control. One version had a series of downward-pointing projections like a coarse-toothed saw and was sometimes called a **ratchet hanger**. One hook usually supported a kettle so that hot water was always available. Tilting a large kettle full of hot water was difficult and potentially hazardous, so a device was invented to do so safely, which is variously described in modern books as an **idle-back**, **lazy-back**, or **lazy susie**, though all these words have other meanings—an *idle-back* was a lazy person, *lazy-back* is a US term for a chair with a reclining back, and *lazy Susan* more commonly refers to that rotating plate in the centre of a table that gives everyone easy access to the condiments.

In addition to the crook-tree, many kitchens had triangular brackets called **chimney-cranes** (the "swinging cranes" of Rand's text) attached to the walls of the hearth. Pots were hung on these. The cranes were on hinges so they could be swung out away from the fire to let the cook get at the pot. Other pots stood in front of the fire on three-legged stands variously called **brandreths** (from Old Norse *brand-reið*, a grate), **brandises** (Old English *brand-ísen*, from *brand*, burning + *ísen*, iron), **brandirons**, or **trivets** (Latin *tri-*, three + *pēs*, foot). The fire itself was in a grate supported by **firedogs** or **andirons** (a mysterious word, this, from Old French *andier*, of unknown origin). Standing nearby would be a long-handled pole with a flat disc at the end, called a **peel** (from Latin *pala*, spade), which the cook used for sliding bread and other items into the brick ovens and getting them out again.

The cooks had **tinder boxes**, containing flint, steel, and tinder with which to relight the fire should it ever go out. They would have been delighted with the convenience of matches, invented only in the 1830s. Early examples were called **Lucifers** (Latin, "light-bringing"), whose name might remind you of the line from the First World War song, "While you've a Lucifer to light your fag", and **Prometheans**, from the Greek god who stole fire back from Zeus and returned it to Earth. But in old kitchens of any size the fire was rarely allowed to go out. Instead, it was allowed to die down at night and servants put a metal cover over the embers to keep it in until the morning. This also acted as a wise fire precaution. The cover was called in French a **couvre-feu** (Anglicized to **cover-fire**), the origin of our **curfew**. Every kitchen had a store of wood, including **faggots**—bundles of sticks tied together—to get the fire blazing up again quickly (the word is from Italian *fagotto*, based on Greek *phakelos*, a bundle).

After the kitchen range became common in the late eighteenth century, most of these blacksmith's items vanished from the kitchen and its appearance started to take on its modern form. An early type of range was called a **kitchener**, a term based on the medieval name of the person who had charge of the kitchen in a monastery. The modern sense survived well into the twentieth century; George Orwell uses it in *The Road to Wigan Pier* in 1937:

> In winter it is so cold that the kitcheners have to
> be kept burning day and night, and the windows,
> needless to say, are never opened.

About 1790, Benjamin Thompson, Count Rumford, improved the kitchen range to reduce the need for fuel and get rid of the smoke. These became known as **Rumford kitchens** or **Rumford stoves**. That explains the reference in Jane Austen's *Northanger Abbey* of 1818:

> The fireplace, where she had expected the ample
> width and ponderous carving of former times,
> was contracted to a Rumford, with slabs of plain
> though handsome marble, and ornaments over it
> of the prettiest English china.

A kitchen that had gone through this process was sometimes said to have been **Rumfordized**.

Among those in the kitchen was the **custron**, a low-born boy who did many of the most menial jobs. His name came from an Old French word meaning a scullion, a later term for the same sort of person. You can tell the work that **scullions** did from the French origin of his name in *escouillon*, a swab or cloth, which in turn derives from *escouvre*, a broom or besom. What looks like a linked word, **scullery**, the room where the dishes were cleaned after meals, is actually from a different source, the Latin *scutella*, a salver; from this came, indirectly via French, yet another name for the same type of menial servant, a **squiller**. An even older term for him was **drivel**, from a Germanic word literally meaning a driver or a tool for driving and which was applied to a turnspit (though it later became a term for an imbecile, the modern derogatory meaning of nonsense is only indirectly connected).

In the **hall** (which then meant the main public room of the building; it has gone down in size and public estimation since those days), the servants included the **ewerer**, who provided guests at table with water to wash their hands; his name came from the jug called a **ewer**, from Latin *aqua*, water, via Old French *ewe*, modern French *eau*. Another was the **sewer**, who organized the table settings, seated the guests, and arranged the serving of the various dishes. *Sewer* had nothing to do with the name for a waste pipe or with sewing clothes—his name was from the Old French *asseour*, to cause to sit, with the initial letters chopped off.

The **acater** (from Old French *acateor*, buyer) was in charge of purchasing all the provisions for the household and his name later similarly lost its beginning to give us *cater* and *caterer*. Those in charge of the provisions he supplied included the **panter**, who supplied the bread for the household and who had charge of the **pantry** (both names come from the same Latin source, *panem*, as the modern French *pain* for bread). Even from early times, the pantry also housed other provisions, but bread was the most important foodstuff. As you might guess, the **cellarer** had charge of the cellar, though his specific job was to look after the wine.

The beer came from the **buttery**. Originally, that had nothing to do with butter, but was the room off the hall, near the pantry, where the **butts** were kept; these were big casks of beer (Old French *bot*, from late Latin *buttis*, cask or wineskin). The man in charge here was the **butler**, at that time a much more lowly servant than the magisterial supervisor of the below-stairs realm he became later. In time, *buttery* became the usual name for a place where various provisions were kept; visitors might call at the buttery-hatch for informal refreshment, as a character was allusively told in Ben Jonson's *Every Man In His Humour* (1598):

> A trencher and a napkin you shall have in the
> buttery.

A **trencher** was either a wooden platter for food or a thick slice of bread used in the same way, though its first sense—from French *trancher*, to cut—was of the knife you cut your food with rather than the base on which you did the cutting; a **trencherman** enjoyed his food, "one who plays a good knife and fork", as the first edition of the *Oxford English Dictionary* put it.

A general term for most of these intermediate grade servants was **yeoman** (possibly from an Old English phrase meaning young man), so the butler might instead be called the **yeoman of the buttery** and the panter the **yeoman of the pantry**. The same word turns up in **yeoman of the revels** (the man in charge of after-dinner entertainment) and in **Yeoman of the Guard** (a member of the sovereign's bodyguard). Later it came to refer to a man with a small landed estate, regarded sentimentally at one time as the backbone of the nation's life in the phrase the **yeomen of England**, as in *A History of English Prose Fiction*, by Bayard Tuckerman:

> The yeomen of England were imbued with a spirit
> of courage and liberty unknown to the same class
> on the continent of Europe, and their love of
> freedom and restless activity of disposition
> found a reflection in the person of their hero.

There were many such titles, including **yeoman fewterer**, the man in charge of the greyhounds (from Latin *vertragum*, greyhound, a word of Celtic origin), the **yeoman garneter**, who was in charge of the granary (Latin *granarium*, which via Old French *gernier* has also bequeathed us *garner*, to gather or collect), and the **yeoman harbinger** (from Old Saxon *heriberga*, lodgings or shelter for an army), who travelled ahead of a nobleman's household to arrange accommodation, from which we get our modern sense of harbinger as something or someone that foreshadows an event.

Many of these old words, as we've seen, have changed their meaning greatly over time. So have others. A **cupboard** was once literally a board—on trestles—on which were laid out the cups and other vessels needed in the kitchen or at table. Similarly a **buffet** (Old French *bufet*, stool) didn't at first refer to a stand-up self-service meal, but to a piece of dining-room furniture with cupboards and open shelves for keeping crockery in (a sense retained in American English). Don't believe anyone who tries to tell you that the servant who waited at the buffet was a *buffetier*, from which derives *Beefeater* for a member of the Yeomen of the Guard: it's rubbish. There was no such word as *buffetier* and **beefeater** was in its origins a dismissive term for a menial person who looked rather too well fed.

At the time of the first Elizabeth a **banquet** might not be a sumptuous feast—though confusingly it could be—but was often a course of sweetmeats, fruit, and wine served after the main dinner was over (*banquet* is from French *banc*, bench, so containing the same idea as our *board* in the sense of a table spread for a meal and so the meal itself, as in *board and lodging*). The physician Thomas Cogan disparaged the practice in his book *The Haven of Health, Made for the Comfort of Students* of 1584:

> Yea, and after supper for fear lest they be not full gorged, to have a delicate banquet, with abundance of wine.

Sometimes it was served in another room, sometimes in a little turret room on the roof, or sometimes even in a separate building. The idea behind consuming it somewhere else was to give time for the hall to be cleared or **voided** for entertainment. The same idea turns up in **dessert**, from French *desservir*, to clear the table.

When a nobleman was out riding, he often had **footmen** with him. These were fit young men who walked or ran alongside the horses and who could race ahead to deliver messages or run errands. They were more fully called **running footmen**. Another name for them was **lackey**, ultimately via French from Arabic *al-qā'id*, the chief, a word that has since gone even further downhill to mean a servile follower; in 1596, Anthony Munday complained in *Sylvain's Orator*

> How many noble men do burst their lackeys legs
> with running.

Only in the eighteenth century did footmen come indoors, to do a lot of the menial jobs and to help the butler serve at table, though they still ran errands.

There were also many **grooms** (originally meaning a young man), a job now restricted to looking after horses but which in late medieval times could refer to any lowly servant. As late as the nineteenth century some English great houses had **grooms of the chamber**, though they had a much higher status by then; those in charge of horses were specifically the **grooms of the stable**. The appearance of *groom* as half of *bridegroom* was a folk error of the fourteenth century—it had earlier been *brȳdguma*, from Old English *guma*, man; when *guma* went out of use, people changed it to the only other word they knew that seemed to make some sense. From the seventeenth century, carriages hauled by four or more horses required **postillions** (from Italian *postiglione*, a guide for someone carrying mail on horseback), though you will be glad to know they were rarely struck by lightning.

Victorian establishments had many jobs for young women, generically called **maids** (an abbreviation of *maiden*), including **lady's maid**, **parlourmaid**, **kitchenmaid**, **housemaid**, **scullery-maid**, **laundry-maid**, and **between-maid**. The last of these combined the duties of a housemaid with those of a kitchenmaid and so regularly moved between the two areas; her name was often abbreviated to **tweeny**; today *tweeny* or *tweenie* is more familiar as a young person between about 8 and 13, a humorously informal term modelled on *teen*. The servants' quarters were usually referred to generically as **below stairs**, because they were often in the basement, though the term was used even when they weren't; **above stairs** was the realm of the family they served. The hardest job of all was the **maid-of-all-work**, who was often the sole servant in a small household and had to do everything.

Among male jobs in the same period was the **valet**, from Latin *vassallus*, a retainer, which was also the origin of **varlet**, an older name for the same function, whose title went badly downhill in the sixteenth century, when it came to mean a rogue or rascal;

from the Latin word also came **vassal**, a medieval holder of land by feudal tenure. An upmarket term for a valet was **gentleman's gentleman**, equivalent in status to the lady's maid, who carried out a great range of duties for his master; the most famous in fiction is P G Wodehouse's brainy servant of the feckless Bertie Wooster; in *Stiff Upper Lip, Jeeves* of 1963 Wodehouse has Bertie remark:

> Jeeves, of course, is a gentleman's gentleman, not a butler, but if the call comes, he can buttle with the best of them.

PART 2

Health
& Medicine

Potions and curatives

BEFORE THE ERA of modern drugs the boundary between foods and medicines was blurred. A wide range of herbs—meaning any product of vegetable origin, including leaves, flowers, seeds, bark, or roots—were thought to ease or cure ailments.

Oliver Wendell Holmes wrote of a medical practitioner in New England in the seventeenth century:

> His pharmacopoeia consisted mainly of simples,
> such as the venerable 'Herball' of Gerard describes
> and figures in abounding affluence.

These **simples** were the individual herbs that were *compounded* as needed to make remedies. **Compound** (from Latin *cum*, with) originally meant a substance made of ingredients literally pounded together; only later did it take on the modern sense of a chemical substance whose elemental components are intimately linked at the atomic level. The pharmacy of an eighteenth- or nineteenth-century hospital would have relied as extensively on herbal remedies as would have a medieval monastery. Drawers and jars would have contained the simples, with the most common medicines made up ready for use.

Among these herbs are many unfamiliar to us today, at least under the names that physicians and apothecaries gave them. **Asarabacca**, from the Greek name for the plant, is a rare British woodland plant, which the herbalists also called *hazelwort*. William Salisbury, in *The Botanist's Companion* of 1818, remarked that its roots and leaves "evacuate powerfully both upwards and downwards", in more stately language to act both as emetics and purgatives. But he went on to say that the herb was then mainly used as a **sternutatory**, a sneeze-provoking remedy to clear the nose (it's from Latin *sternuere*, to sneeze) or an **errhine** (Greek *errinon*, in the nostril), another name for the same thing. Asarabacca is a relative of **birthwort**; as the name shows, that herb was once given as an aid to childbirth, and also to induce abortion.

Eryngo or **eryngium** is an old name for sea holly, from its Greek name. In *The Complete Herbal*, Nicholas Culpeper says:

> The plant is venereal, and breeds seed
> exceedingly, and strengthens the spirit
> procreative.

But he says it can treat other conditions, including one adverse result of the procreative spirit, the **French pox** or syphilis (which the French, in a spirit of entente cordiale, called the *English disease*), which was also known at the time as **crinkum** or **grincome**, as in **crinkum-krankum**, a narrow twisting passage, a word applied in low slang to the vagina. Culpeper said that eryngo also cured **imposthumes** or abscesses, a word much messed about with during its passage from Greek via Latin *apostema* and French into English. Another reputed aphrodisiac that Culpeper mentioned was **satyrion** (from the Greek word that has also bequeathed us *satyr*), a name given to various varieties of orchids. It's not accidental that these plants owe their name to Greek *orkhis*, testicle, because of the shape of their tubers.

Mandragora is an old name, now only poetic, for the root of the mandrake plant, once considered a useful narcotic, which often turns up as an echo of Iago's words in Shakespeare's *Othello*:

> Not poppy nor mandragora
> Nor all the drowsy syrups of the world
> Shall ever medicine thee to that sweet sleep
> Which thou own'dst yesterday.

The water germander (once called *garlick germander*, because it smelled of garlic) was also called **scordium**, as it was in classical Greek. It was cultivated in English gardens for its medicinal properties, because it was thought to be an antidote for poisons and an antiseptic; **diascordium** or **diascord** was a compound of scordium with many other herbs, including cinnamon, dittany, tormentil, opium, sorrel seeds, pepper, and ginger.

These last two names include the prefix **dia-** which was taken from the Greek word meaning "through" or "by", and which was attached by physicians from the fifteenth century onwards to the names of substances to mark a medicinal preparation in which the substance was the main ingredient. **Diachylon**, for example, was an ointment made of vegetable juices (it's from Greek *dia chylon*, composed of juices) that included linseed, fenugreek seeds, and the roots of marshmallow, though in the nineteenth century the name was given instead to a widely-used lead-based medical plaster. **Diagrydium** was a purgative made of **scammony**, the dried roots of a member of the convolvulus family (*grydium* may be from a Greek word for the plant). **Diamoron** (from *moron*, the Greek word for the black mulberry; our sense of a stupid person is from a different Greek word, *mõros*), was a preparation made from syrup and mulberry juice that was given to ease sore throats. Among other senses, a **diatessaron** was a medicine made of four ingredients (Greek *dia tessaron*, composed of four), but especially one containing gentian, laurel leaves, myrrh, and birthwort that was considered a useful **alexipharmic** (from Greek words meaning "to ward off poison"), an antidote against poisons. **Diacodium** was an opiate syrup made from poppy-heads, whose name includes the Greek word *kodeia* for the head.

Spignel, a member of the parsley family that went around under several aliases, being also called **baldmoney**, **bearwort**, and **meum** (from its Greek name, *meon*), was a **carminative** that relieved flatulence by expelling gases (this last word comes ultimately from Latin *carminare*, to comb out wool, the old idea being that a carminative unknotted the humours of the body to permit the wind to escape). The **spattling-poppy** that we know better today as bladder campion got its name because it encouraged patients to salivate (*spattle* is an obsolete Old English verb meaning to spit). The lesser celandine was once called the **pile-wort** or **figwort**, since physicians believed it helped relieve piles or haemorrhoids (the *fig* in the second name came about because haemorrhoids were thought to look like figs). **Calamus aromaticus** may have been imported lemon grass but was more likely to have been the native sweet rush (Culpeper includes it in a list of native root simples and says it "provokes the menses" and was, yet again, good as a purgative).

Opopanax is now mostly a constituent of perfumes, but as its Greek name suggests (it means "all-healing juice") it was once thought medically valuable; it was a resin that might have been from a parsnip-like plant of southern Europe but was more probably from the native lovage. **Biting arsmart** or **arsesmart** (so called, as John Minsheu explained in a book of 1617: "Because if it touch the taile or other bare skinne, it maketh it smart", i.e. sting) is now more commonly called water pepper. It gained its effect from the acrid oils in its sap and it had many uses, including killing fleas. Culpeper says of it that it was "an admirable remedy for the gout, being roasted between two tiles and applied to the grieved place"; it was distinguished by some herbalists from **mild arsesmart**, a related plant. **Hypocistis**, often mentioned in the pharmacology of the seventeenth century as a tonic and astringent, is the juice of a southern European parasitic plant (it grows on the roots of species of *Cistus*, rock roses, hence the name).

Though many herbs were native, others travelled great distances to reach English physicians. **Mechoacan**, named after the Mexican province from which it was imported, was the root of a type of bindweed that was used as a purgative. **Sagapenum** was a gum obtained from a plant of the Middle East that was used as an **emmenagogue**, a substance that stimulates or increases menstrual flow (it's from Greek *emmena*, menses). On its arrival from the New World in 1529, **cocoa** (whose name came via Spanish from Nahuatl *cacaua*) soon gained a reputation for curing the **wasting disease**, an old name for tuberculosis. When **tobacco** appeared in the following century, it was for a while lauded for curing everything from bad breath to chilblains to fatigue. Its name was introduced to English via Spanish *tabaco* from a word in either the Carib or Taino languages, or just possibly from Arabic—the experts disagree.

We are appalled these days at the apparently casual way in which physicians used substances we consider to be deadly poisons. Mercury was a classic case. As a vapour and in various compounds it was for some four hundred years a notorious treatment for syphilis, one with reason often considered worse than the original disease. In the nineteenth century, a controversy separated doctors who continued to advocate mercury treatment from those who opposed it, dubbed respectively **mercuralists** and **non-mercuralists**. In the eighteenth century, **aethiops mineral** was a preparation of mercury and sulphur ground together to make a black powder (hence *aethiops*, from the Latin word for a black-faced person from which we get *Ethiopian*); it was used to treat eye inflammations and intestinal disorders. From the late eighteenth century onwards, people were prescribed **blue pills** containing mercury to cure constipation. **Turpeth** or **turbith mineral** was a lemon-yellow form of mercury sulphate, another purgative and emetic; the latter name distinguished it from **turbith vegetable**, the root of an Indian plant that has similarly been used as a purgative (all these words are from the Arabic and Persian name for the plant, *turbi*).

Another treatment for constipation was the **black draught**, an all too effective purgative, to judge from Mrs Beeton's recipe for it:

> Infusion of senna 10 drachms; Epsom salts 10
> drachms; tincture of senna, compound tincture

> of cardamums, compound spirit of lavender, of
> each 1 drachm.

Doctors faced with a particularly difficult case, or those with sadistic impulses, might have added **colocynth**, the pulp of the fruits of the bitter-apple (from the plant's Greek name, *kolokunthis*) which supplied another powerful purgative. In July 1890, *Punch* included it in a verse mocking the tomato-based treatment for indigestion that had originally been advocated by the American Dr John Cook Bennett in 1835:

> Don't talk to me of colocynth or famed cerulean
> pill,
> Don't mention hyoscyamus or aloes when I'm ill;
> The very word podophyllin is odious in mine ears,
> The thought of all the drugs I've ta'en calls up the
> blinding tears;
> The Demon of Dyspepsia, a sufferer writes to say,
> At sight of the Tomato-plant will vanish quite
> away.

Cerulean pill was a poetic term—if such a thing were possible—for the infamous blue pill; **hyoscyamus** was an extract of henbane, whose biological name is *Hyoscyamus niger* (it's from Greek words meaning "pig bean"); it was more commonly a sedative or a treatment for what were then called nervous diseases rather than a purgative; **podophyllin** or **podophyllum** (Greek *podus*, foot + *phyllon*, leaf) was another folk purgative, now banned for internal use, obtained from the rhizomes of a plant Americans know as the mayapple or American henbane. An even more drastic purgative was **croton oil**, extracted from the seeds of a tropical Asian tree; it was so foul that, on the old wives' principle that if something is awful it will surely do you good, it must have been a powerfully curative elixir.

Caudles, cordials, and possets

SEEMING TO REFUTE that old wives' tale, certain types of bland foodstuffs were also considered to be especially efficacious in times of sickness.

Speaking once more of Patrick O'Brian's creation Stephen Maturin, like so many physicians, he is proving a difficult patient in *HMS Surprise*, not least when presented with things that are intended to do him good:

> It is another of your damned possets. Am I in childbed, for all love, that I should be plagued, smothered, destroyed with caudle?

A **posset** was prepared from milk curdled with ale, wine, or other liquor, usually with sugar, spices, and herbs added in and served hot. Culpeper mentions one made with leeks; Elizabeth Moxon in 1764 suggests recipes with almonds or lemons; others refer to nutmegs, treacle, and other ingredients; Elizabeth

Gaskell writes in *Half a Life-Time Ago* in 1855 of **treacle-posset** as "the homely country remedy against an incipient cold". Samuel Pepys always writes of eating a posset rather than drinking one, implying they were served thick; these were sometimes called **eating possets**. The most common type was **sack-posset**, made with the wine called sack, though Sir Walter Scott mentions **brandy posset**. The **cardus posset** was made with the milk thistle (Latin *carduus*), long believed to be a remedy for liver problems. Two for special occasions were **birth-posset** (to restore the mother, not to give to the baby) and **bride-posset** (drunk in the nuptial chamber). A child's bedtime drink might be a **sleepy posset**. Possets had been common for centuries—the finer varieties, made with wine and spices and enriched with cream, were served at formal suppers in the eighteenth century—but by the Napoleonic period of Patrick O'Brian's books they were usually regarded as invalid food. Nobody seems to know where *posset* came from, but the *Oxford English Dictionary* suggests it might be linked to *posca*, a Latin term for a mixture of vinegar and water or vinegar and wine.

Another word for *posset* in the fifteenth century was **balductum** (from Latin *balducta*, curds), a word that later took on the sense of a farrago of nonsense, or of something trashy or rubbishy. Dr Maturin's opinion of the stuff clearly wasn't new. Another name, two centuries later, was **merribowk** or **merrybouk** (probably *merry* + *bouk*, from Old English *búc*, belly, so *merry belly*, a fine name for a pleasant dish). A more familiar name today is **syllabub** (origin uncertain, but the ending may again be from Old English *búc*), a similar creation known from the sixteenth century, whose principal characteristic was its foaming head. It went out of favour in the nineteenth century but has now been revived in a small way as a dessert. In the eighteenth century *syllabub* became yet another disparaging term, this time for writing that was as unsubstantial and frothy as the dish itself.

The **caudle** that Dr Maturin disparages was also a warm drink, but this time based on gruel, mixed with ale or wine to which spices, sugar, or honey were added. The word derives from the Latin *calidus*, warm, from which we also get *calorie* and *chowder* and which turns up, much disguised, in *nonchalant*, for someone who doesn't get hot under the collar. **Caudle ferry** was a favourite dish in medieval times, which had breadcrumbs added and was yellow because of the egg yolks added to thicken it; reputedly it was often thick enough to cut into slices (nobody knows for sure where *ferry* comes from, though Old French had *feré*, relating to a festival, suggesting that caudle ferry was originally intended for a special occasion). **Ale caudles** were likewise often made with breadcrumbs and eggs.

A later use for caudles was as a sort of custard as a filling for pies and tarts, usually with a mixture of wine or verjuice, egg yolks, and butter. In the seventeenth century the **tea caudle** was invented as a way to consume this expensive new drink from China. The philosopher, courtier, and early scientific experimenter Sir Kenelm Digby wrote in 1669:

> Take two yolks of new-laid eggs, and beat them
> very well with as much fine sugar as sufficient for
> the quantity of liquor; when they are very well
> incorporated, pour your tea upon the eggs and
> sugar, and stir them well together. So drink it hot.

As Stephen Maturin's outburst suggests, caudles were commonly given to sick people and especially to women at the time of childbirth. Near the start of the nineteenth century the verb *coddle* was created from *caudle*; it was later extended to *mollycoddle*, using *molly* in its disparaging slang sense of a milksop or effeminate man (**molly-houses** in the eighteenth century were meeting places for homosexuals). An entry in the first edition (1870) of Brewer's *Dictionary of Phrase and Fable* (no longer present) suggests that the late Dr Ebenezer Cobham Brewer shared Dr Maturin's detestation, describing the caudle as

> any sloppy mess, especially that sweet mixture of
> gruel and wine or spirits once given by nurses to
> recently confined women and their "gossips" who
> called to see the baby during the first month.

Gossips' cup was indeed once a type of caudle.

In the US in the nineteenth century this association of caudles with new babies was formalized with **caudle parties**.

"Nowadays," remarked Mrs Sherwood in a strained bit of prose in her *Manners and Social Usages* of 1887,

> a caudle party is a very gay, dressy affair, and
> given about six weeks after young master or
> mistress is ready to be congratulated or condoled
> with on his or her entrance upon this mundane
> sphere.

Though the custom continued, the recipe seems to change: Emily Post noted in her famous book *Etiquette* of 1922 that

> although according to cook-books caudle is a
> gruel, the actual 'caudle' invariably served at
> christenings is a hot eggnog, drunk out of little
> punch cups.

A century before, the cups would have been specifically called **caudle cups**; these were small, often of silver, with covers and two handles so they could easily be passed from person to person.

The third set of medicinal substances that were very familiar to Dr Maturin were the **cordials**. These were infusions of spirits with herbs, or mixtures of such ingredients subsequently re-distilled. They were originally called **cordial waters**, whose name came from the Latin word for heart (also the origin of the figurative sense of *cordial*, "sincere, genuine, warm"); many of them were called **waters** instead. They were thought to invigorate the heart and stimulate the circulation and were frequently sweetened with sugar or sugar syrup and often brightly coloured by extracts of rose leaves and the like.

They are linked through the alcohol and colour to **tinctures**, which were at first dyes or colouring matters (the name comes from the Latin *tingere*, to dye or colour, which also gives us our *tint*, *tinge*, and *taint*). Alchemists came to mean by *tincture* the essential qualities of a substance that had been taken into solution. This later led to the more modern pharmaceutical sense of a solution of a substance in alcohol (and to the slang sense of *tincture*, attributed falsely by John Wells in *Private Eye* to the late Sir Denis Thatcher, of a spirituous beverage of some kind, a "snifter"). The medicinal preparations of this sort once included the **sacred tincture**, one of many drugs given to Charles II in his last days, which contained aloes and rhubarb. The **thebaic tincture** (Latin *Thebaicus*, of Thebes in Egypt) was a tincture of opium, so named because Egypt was anciently an important source of that drug. Another name for a tincture of opium was **laudanum**, a word invented by the medieval Swiss physician Paracelsus. **Huxham's tincture** was created by the English physician John Huxham (1692–1768) and contained cinchona bark; it was used as a bitter tonic and to reduce fever. **Warburg's tincture** was a proprietary medicine that included quinine, invented by a doctor of that name in London, but popular in the US for many decades in the nineteenth century.

Cordials were sold by distillers, doctors, and apothecaries and were once commonly made in the still-houses or still-rooms of the larger domestic establishments (the ability to distil liquors was once regarded as an essential accomplishment of an upper-class housewife, though later it was taken over by the housekeeper). There were dozens of different types. An early example, from the sixteenth century, was **rosa solis** (Latin, "rose of the sun") or **rosolio**, which was flavoured with the insectivorous plant sundew. John Gerard wrote in his *Herball* of 1597 that it should contain "Cinnamon, Cloves, Maces, Ginger, Nutmegs, Sugar, and a few grains of Muske" as well as sundew. It was said to "stir up lust" and was regarded as an aphrodisiac. Another was **usquebaugh** (Gaelic *uisge*, water + *beatha*, life, a direct translation of the Latin *aqua vitae*); the word is the source of our modern *whisky* and *whiskey*, but in the 1600s and 1700s it was a cordial, for which there were many recipes. They had in common a base of French brandy, plus fennel, liquorice, aniseed, coriander, and saffron, with raisins and figs to add sweetness. In *The Orators* in 1762, the playwright Samuel Foote called it "an exhilirator of the bowels, and a stomatic to the head" (a **stomatic** confusingly not being a medicine for the stomach but one that was good for oral diseases, from Greek *stoma*, mouth).

In *The Art of Distillation* in 1651, John French lists many cordials that were thought to be specifics against disease, including **Dr Burges' plague water** and the **palsy water** of Dr Mathias.

Another was **Dr Steven's Water**, for which John French gave a recipe:

> Take a gallon of gascoigne wine; a dram each of
> ginger, galganal, cinnamon, nutmeg, grains,
> aniseed, fennel seeds, carroway seeds; a handful
> each of sage, red mints, red roses, thyme,
> pellitory, rosemary, wild thyme, chamomile, and
> lavender.

The mixture was then distilled.

Most cordials were less complex. They included **angelica water** (proof spirit re-distilled with the herb angelica, which Culpeper praised: "It comforts the heart, cherishes the vital spirits, resists the pestilence, and all corrupt airs, which indeed are the natural causes of epidemical diseases"); **lavender water** (at one time taken internally against **falling sickness**, an old name for epilepsy, and against infirmities of the brain); **surfeit water** (poppies, raisins, and spices infused in distilled alcohol or re-distilled; so called because it was thought to cure a surfeit of eating and drinking); **hysterical water** (good for women's complaints, *hysterical* being from Greek *hystera*, womb); and **clary water** (which was distilled using the flowers of the plant we now call wild clary, a relative of sage). **Diamber** was made with ambergris and musk; in medieval Latin *diambra* was ambergris, the prefix *dia-* denoting a medicinal compound, as I said earlier, and *ambra* being the old word for ambergris, from French *ambre gris*, literally "grey amber", to distinguish it from *ambre jaune*, "yellow amber", the fossil sap of trees. Other cordials included **confectio alkermes** or **alkermes syrup** (containing the dried bodies of the *kermes* or scarlet grain insect), **ratafia** (brandy infused with almonds or apricot or cherry kernels, not the aperitif of unfermented champagne grape juice mixed with brandy which is its meaning today), and **saffron cordial** (which used marigold flowers, nutmeg, and saffron). Others were based on cinnamon, caraway, cloves, **bigarades** (a Spanish bitter orange), and treacle.

After his diatribe against possets and caudles, Dr Maturin also dismisses with a shudder **Godfrey's cordial**. This was originally prepared by Thomas Godfrey of Hunsdown in Hertfordshire in the early eighteenth century. It was a tincture of opium with sassafras and treacle that remained popular through the nineteenth century and well into the twentieth; the *Dictionary of National Biography* says

> Its sweetness and agreeable flavour, added to its
> ability to knock out or at least dull the senses of
> the most fractious patient, made it a boon for
> distraught mothers and lazy nurses.

(Nurses had an especially bad reputation: in 1860, Wilkie Collins noted in *The Woman in White* that hired nurses were "proverbially as cruel a set of women as are to be found in all England".) A report to the Children's Employment Commissioners for the town of Dudley in 1841 said:

> Godfrey's Cordial is not much used here by the
> mothers of infants; but they give the children,
> instead of this, a mixture of chalk and laudanum,
> called **Atkinson's Infant Preservative**.
> Sometimes they give the infants pain-easing
> Drops, which are nothing but laudanum in
> tincture. This is done to put them to sleep while
> the mother goes out all day to work. They also
> administer **Dalby's Carminative**—a mixture very
> like Atkinson's.

Many other proprietary or patent medicines of the eighteenth and nineteenth centuries were similarly called cordials, including **Dr Brodum's Nervous Cordial** (William Brodum's real name was probably Issachar Cohen; he also sold his **botanical syrup** as a cure for scurvy); **Mr Cornwell's Oriental Vegetable Cordial** ("especially efficacious against excruciating pains in the bowels"); **Dr Solomon's Cordial Balm of Gilead** ("In inward decays, debility, and lowness of spirits, its merits stand unequalled"; launched by Samuel Solomon in 1796, it was a mixture of old brandy laced with herbs); and **Van Swieten's Gout Cordial**. We know little about what went into many of them, though alcohol certainly featured strongly. Americans scornfully came to know similar products of quackery as **snake oil remedies** because in the late nineteenth century in the US their proprietors claimed to have based them on an oil derived from rattlesnakes, though they were really coloured and flavoured mineral oils.

In the Victorian period, under the influence of the temperance movement, some drinks described as non-alcoholic cordials (a contradiction in terms) were created to refresh the inner person without causing inebriation. In *Gaslight and Daylight* of 1859, George Augustus Sala mentions an American ship's captain who drank non-alcoholic **raspberry cordial** and noted:

> All publics [that is, public houses] frequented by those who go down to the sea in ships keep a store of this, and similar cordials, such as **gingerette**, **lemonette**, **orangette**, all mixing with sugar and hot water in a duly groggy manner, but all perfectly innocuous and teetotal.

Henry Mayhew, in *London Labour and the London Poor* of 1851, refers to **raspberryette**, another drink of similar kind, a sort of non-alcoholic alcopop. Temperance influence led to *cordial* coming to refer to various beverages with no implication of alcohol, so that by the time of my youth in the 1940s the word could refer to any coloured, flavoured, and sweetened non-alcoholic glop.

Of course, alcoholic cordials never went out of fashion and the confusion with temperance drinks sometimes made it easy for backsliding takers of the pledge to continue their old habits. From the middle of the eighteenth century, however, another name for them began to be used: **liqueur** (from the French word for liquor). The move from *cordial* to *liqueur* was undoubtedly hastened by the later confusion with temperance drinks but also because such drinks moved in public regard from being medicinal to recreational. Most of the drinks then called liqueurs—whose names mostly appeared in the language in the nineteenth century—are still with us, such as **absinthe**, **Benedictine**, **chartreuse**, **curaçao**, **Grand Marnier**, and **kümmel**, a surprising number of which had their origins in monasteries.

Other restorative drinks in earlier centuries were based on ale. In the eighteenth century these were grouped under the heading of **physical ales** (the first word being from *physic*, the art of healing). **Covent-garden purl** was a purging drink made with coriander seeds, senna, rosemary and sage flowers, and wormwood. **Scurvygrass-ale** or **scurvy-ale** was infused with scurvy grass; it was drunk in spring when the new shoots appeared to cure the deficiency disease caused by a poor winter diet lacking in vitamin C. John Locke wrote in his diary in 1679 that he knew of several compounded ales; as well as scurvygrass-ale he named **cock-ale**. This was as much a food as a drink, being ale mixed with the jelly or minced meat of a boiled cock, plus other ingredients such as raisins and dates. It's often advanced to explain the etymologically mysterious and characteristically American drink called the **cocktail**, but there's nothing we can point at to connect the two drinks other than the similarity in name.

The parlance of physicians

THE OBSCURE LANGUAGE of physicians has been much mocked down the centuries; many of their terms have vanished from everyday life, as have the curatives they referred to.

> I swear by Apollo the physician and Æsculapius and Health and All-Heal and all the gods and goddesses.

This was how on graduating doctors once swore the **Hippocratic Oath** (from *Hippocrates*, the ancient Greek physician who is traditionally regarded as the father of medicine) by which they agreed to observe the obligations of their craft.

All-heal is the exact English equivalent of *Panacea*. She was the daughter of Æsculapius, the Roman god of healing, and her name comes from Greek *panakes*, all-healing. Finding the **panacea**, the universal remedy to all ills, was one aim of medieval alchemy, along with turning base metals into gold (by means of the **philosopher's stone**), discovering a way to live for ever (through the **elixir of life**), and finding the **alkahest** or universal solvent, whose name is fake Arabic. (An ancient riddle poses the question, if you ever managed to create the universal solvent, what would you keep it in?) *All-heal* is also a variant name of several common English plants thought to have particularly strong healing powers, such as valerian and mistletoe. Another name for a panacea in use in the seventeenth century was **panchreston**, from the classical Latin term *panchrestum medica-mentum*, a sovereign remedy, which is from the Greek *panchreston*, something good for everything.

In particular, physicians sought a general antidote to poison, of which one supposedly all-effective type was called a **mithridate**. It was named after Mithridates VI, the king of Pontus, a small kingdom on the southern shore of the Black Sea, who fought four wars with Rome, finally being defeated by Pompey in 65 BC. Mithridates is said to have protected himself against poison by taking progressively larger amounts of the ones that he knew about until he was able to tolerate lethal doses. There are many recipes for mithridates in the old herbals, often extremely complicated. One by Culpeper begins "Take of Myrrh, Saffron, Agarick, Ginger, Cinnamon, Spikenard, Frankincense, Treacle, Mustard seeds ..." and goes on to list 41 other ingredients, many of them extremely rare.

Another poison antidote was a **treacle**, which was supposedly particularly effective against snakebites as well as poisons and malignant diseases. The word can be traced back to Greek *theriake*, antidote against venom, from *therion*, wild beast. It was only at the end of the seventeenth century that *treacle* became the thick, dark syrup that we know now, and the old sense continued in use alongside it for at least another century. Before then it was a salve, created like a mithridate from many ingredients. Some were sweetened with honey and the mental association of sweetness with this medicine may be the reason the word so fundamentally changed its sense. Poor people called anything they used as a sovereign remedy against illness a treacle—in 1727 Richard Bradley's *Family Dictionary* included the comment that

> To eat Garlick fasting is the Treacle of the Country
> People in the time of a Plague.

Some early English translations of the Bible used *treacle* or its variant **triacle** (which, incidentally, shows how *treacle* was once pronounced) where later ones preferred *balm*. There were many sorts of treacle, often named after the places in which they had been created, of which the best known was **Venice treacle**. Harrison Ainsworth includes a vivid description of a physician attempting to treat a case of plague in his *Old St Paul's* of 1841:

> Bloundel was at no loss how to act, but, rubbing
> the part affected with a stimulating ointment, he
> administered at the same time doses of

> mithridate, Venice treacle, and other potent
> alexipharmics.

A **theriac** (from the same Greek root as *treacle*) was often specifically an antidote to the bite of a viper and it was frequently considered necessary to include the snake's flesh as an ingredient.

Yet another prized antidote to poison was the **bezoar**, still the standard term for a type of hard concretion of hair or vegetable fibre that forms naturally in the stomachs of ruminant animals. Belief in its near-magical properties was once common. The word is Persian (*pādzahr*, counter-poison or antidote) and the bezoar's fame as a cure for poison spread westwards from there in medieval times. You swallowed it, or occasionally rubbed it on the infected part. In *A Voyage to Abyssinia*, written by Father Lobo in the eighteenth century, he says:

> I had recourse to bezoar, a sovereign remedy
> against these poisons, which I always carried
> about me.

An **electuary** was a medicinal paste made of various ingredients pounded up with honey to make it more palatable, whose name probably derives from Greek *ekleikhein*, to lick up. (However, medicines that were intended to be licked were called **lambitives**, from Latin *lambere*, to lick.) Electuaries had many uses. In his *Life of Johnson*, James Boswell reproduces a letter

by Samuel Johnson dated 1775 in which he gives a cure for
rheumatism:

> Take equal quantities of flour of sulphur, and
> flour of mustard-seed, make them an electuary
> with honey or treacle; and take a bolus as big as a
> nutmeg several times a day, as you can bear it.

(As befits a lexicographer well acquainted with language change,
Dr Johnson is using the then new sugar-related sense of *treacle*. A
bolus is a small rounded mass of a substance, from the Latin word
for a clod of earth.) Some physicians gilded their electuaries,
which did nothing to help the patient, but wonderfully aided the
doctor because of the extra fees he could charge. Samuel Pepys
several times recorded in his *Diary* taking a "walnut quantity" of
a bolus to help his constipation, though he never says what was
in it.

In the same entry, for 12 October 1663, Pepys records another
attempt to relive his **costive** condition (from Latin *constipare*, to
press together, which is also the source of *constipated*):

> Anon, about 8 o'clock, my wife did give me a
> clyster which Mr Hollyard directed, viz, a pint of
> strong ale, 4 oz of sugar, and 2 oz of butter.

Clyster is an archaic word for what we would now call an enema.
It's from Greek *kluster*, a syringe, from *kluzein*, to wash out.

Pepys may have previously tried a **minorative** (Latin *minorare*, to diminish), some gently laxative medicine. In *Gargantua and Pantagruel*, by François Rabelais, appears this description of one taken by the giant Pantagruel:

> I let pass how for a minorative or gentle potion he took four hundred pound weight of colophoniac scammony, six score and eighteen cartloads of cassia, an eleven thousand and nine hundred pound weight of rhubarb, besides other confuse jumblings of sundry drugs.

Colophoniac is an exceedingly rare adjective referring to a finishing stroke or crowning touch, related to *colophon*, from Greek *kolophon*, a summit or finishing touch, originally an inscription that was placed at the end of a book; **scammony** is a plant whose roots yield a drastic purgative; **cassia** bark was at one time also used as a laxative.

In the works of the medieval physician Paracelsus (his proper name, by the way, was Theophrastus Phillipus Aureolus Bombastus von Hohenheim, which makes us all glad there's a short way to identify him; it's sometimes said falsely that *bombastic* comes from his name, because he was arrogant and dismissive of the doctors of his day), he describes an **opodeldoc**, a word he seems to have conjured up from heaven knows where. For him it was a type of medicinal plaster and the term appears in English until the seventeenth century with that sense. After that, it shifted dramatically to refer to various sorts of liniment based on soap (though one type included opium). A typical use was the one Mrs Beeton recommended for a sprain in her *Book of Household Management* of 1861:

> The joint is to be rubbed twice a day with flannel dipped in opodeldoc, a flannel bandage rolled tightly round the joint, the pressure being greatest at the lowest part, and the patient allowed to walk about with the assistance of a crutch or stick.

A once-famous type was **Dr Steer's Opodeldoc**, made from Castile soap, camphor, oils of marjoram and rosemary, alcohol, and ammonia. It was advertised thus in the *Times* in 1790:

> The efficacy of this medicine in the Rheumatism, Lumbago, Bruises, Sprains, Cramps, &c. is universally acknowledged: it is equally serviceable in Numbness, Stiffness, and Weakness of the Joints, and in restoring a proper Circulation to the Limbs when in a Paralytic state. It is also excellent for Burns and Scalds, as well as for the Sting of venomous Insects.

It goes on to remark that "It is the best embrocation for Horses that are wrung in the Withers."

Another old term for an embrocation or liniment is **cerate** (from the Latin word for wax). This was a stiff oily ointment, made from wax mixed with oil, lard, and medicinal ingredients. It was variable: a home remedy from the US in 1875 for treating blisters included lard, mutton-tallow, beeswax, and sweet oil in its ingredients. One famous type that century was **Turner's cerate**, named after the London physician and expert on skin diseases Daniel Turner (1667–1741); it was a zinc and calamine ointment mixed with olive oil and unsalted butter, regarded as excellent for treating burns; the American *Household Cyclopedia* of 1881 noted that "This ointment is known by the vulgar name of Turners' cerate, as curing the wounds of [wood] Turners", a rare case of a popular etymology depending solely on misplacing an apostrophe.

Among other general terms no longer in doctors' vocabulary are a set that end in *-agogue*, which derive from Greek *agōgos*, leading, and referred to a substance that induced the expulsion of something from the body, such as the *emmenagogue* mentioned earlier (*see page 57*). A **melanagogue** (Greek *melas*, black) was a medicine that was intended to expel black bile. **Black bile** or **black choler** (Greek *kholē*, bile) in medieval medicine was one of the four fluids or **humours** of the body, the others being *blood*, *phlegm*, and *choler*. From these we get our names for what were once thought to be the four main temperaments, each related to the humour that predominated: *melancholic* (from black bile), *sanguine* (from the Latin word for blood), *phlegmatic*, and *choleric* (bad-tempered or irritable, from *choler*). When we say somebody is in a good or bad humour it comes directly from this idea.

So a **cholagogue** was a medicine that carried off bile or choler, in particular one thought to be effective against fevers; it features in an American novel of 1899, *The Cromptons*, by Mary J Holmes:

> If there was any disease for which Peter had a
> special aversion it was malaria, which he fancied
> he knew how to treat, having had it once himself.
> Quinine, cholagogue, and whiskey were
> prescribed in large quantities.

A **panchymagogue** (from Greek *pan*, all + *chyma*, a fluid or humour) was a universal purge for all the morbid or unhealthy humours of the body. One condition in which there was thought to be a fault in the humours was often described as **adust**, with the state known as **adustion**, the symptoms being a dry and hot body, thirst, a burnt colour of the blood, and a melancholic complexion. Or the patient might have been suffering from **cacochymy** (from a Greek word meaning having unhealthy humours), an ill-humoured state.

Other terms were taken directly from the Latin and Greek which physicians often spoke among themselves. A **stegnotic** was a medicine that helped to arrest a flow of blood or other discharges (from Greek *stegnos*, something watertight or costive). An **apozem** was a decoction or infusion (from Greek *apozema*, from a verb meaning to boil), particularly an opening medicine for the bowels, which seems to have sometimes been all too effective, to judge from a reference in *Sir Launcelot Greaves*, which Tobias Smollett wrote in 1762:

> To be sure his apozem has had a blessed
> effect—five-and-twenty stools since three
> o'clock in the morning.

A **digerent** (Latin *digere*, to digest) medicine or agent promoted digestion or suppuration, while a **catagmatic** one (Greek *katagma*, breakage or fracture) helped to heal fractures. To **mundify** was to free the body, or some part of it, such as a wound, from noxious matter, to cleanse or purify it (from Latin *mundus*, clean). A **deoppilant** (Latin *oppilare*, to stop up) or a **deobstruent** (Latin *obstruere*, to obstruct) was a medicine that removed obstructions by opening the natural passages or pores of the body, whilst a **corroborant** was an invigorating medicine, a tonic.

Among medical instruments the most famous or notorious was the **fleam**, a sharp tool or lancet used to open a vein during **phlebotomy**, the letting of blood, once considered a vital tool in improving the health of a patient by removing corrupt or bad blood so that the patient's body could replace it by good. Both words ultimately derive from the Greek word for a vein. The practice often didn't find favour with patients; a doughty opponent appears in Charles Reade's *Peg Woffington*:

> Sir Charles recovered his reason, so much so, that
> when the chirurgeon approached with his fleam
> to bleed him, according to the practice of the

> day, the patient drew his sword, and assured the
> other he would let out every drop of blood in his
> body if he touched him.

(**Chirurgeon** is an older form of our *surgeon*, both words coming from Greek *kheirourgia*, handiwork or surgery, which contains the elements *kheir*, hand, and *ergon*, work.)

Another method was called **cupping**, in which a piece of paper soaked in alcohol was set alight inside a cup or **cupping-glass**. This was immediately applied to skin on which shallow incisions had been made by a **scarificator** so that the partial vacuum in the cup caused by the burning flame would draw out blood. A Minnesota newspaper in 1886 told of a doctor attempting to treat a man bitten by a rabid dog:

> With a knife from my pocketcase [I] made the
> parts bleed freely wherever the teeth had
> entered, and by means of a tumbler and a little
> spirits of wine extemporized a cupping-glass.

Other instruments unfamiliar to us today include the **Alphonsin** (named after its sixteenth-century inventor, Alphonsus Ferrier of Naples), which had three elastic branches, designed to extract bullets, and the **pulsilogium**, an early pulse-measuring device reputedly invented by Sanctorius of Padua. It was in essence a pendulum—the physician adjusted the length of its cord until the swings matched the patient's pulse; the length of the cord was taken as the measure.

A common method of diagnosis, practised since classical times, was to study the patient's urine, even to the extent of tasting it. It's not as daft as it sounds, since—for example—a sweet taste was an indication of diabetes. As a result, slangy terms for physicians included **piss-prophet**, **water-caster**, and **waterologer**, though all were equally directed at quack doctors.

Another term for a physician was **leech**. Since one method of treatment was to apply the blood-sucking worms called leeches to supposedly draw out the bad humours of the body, it's often assumed this is also disrespectful. But the two terms are completely unrelated. This sense of *leech* is from an ancient Germanic word for a doctor or physician, which is the source of the Old English **leechcraft** for the art of healing. By analogy, at one time a **dog-leech** was a vet, though it was also yet another pejorative word for a quack doctor. The ring finger was once called the **leech-finger** (also the **medical finger** and **physic finger**), a translation of the Latin *digitus medicus*. It's not certain how it got that name, though some writers say it was because the vein that pulsed in it was believed to communicate directly with the heart and so gave that finger healing properties, for example in mixing ointments.

One term that's definitely pejorative is **quack**. It's an abbreviation of an old Dutch word that in the modern language is spelled *kwakzalver* but in English usually appeared as **quacksalver** (from old Dutch *quack*, a person who chatters or prattles, probably connected to the noise a duck makes, and *salf*, essentially the same as *salve*). A quacksalver boasted about the virtues of his remedies and the word later became attached to a person who falsely claimed to know of or who sold miraculous medications. One came in for a tongue-lashing in Sir Walter Scott's *The Fair Maid of Perth*:

> Thou walking skeleton! thou asthmatic gallipot! thou poisoner by profession! if I thought that the puff of vile breath thou hast left could blight for the tenth part of a minute the fair fame of Catharine Glover, I would pound thee, quacksalver! in thine own mortar, and beat up thy wretched carrion with flower of brimstone, the only real medicine in thy booth, to make a salve to rub mangy hounds with!

(A **gallipot** was a small pot made from glazed earthenware or metal that pharmacists used to hold medicines or ointments, probably called that because they came from the Mediterranean in galleys. **Brimstone** is the old name for sulphur.) Mercury was then called **quicksilver**, because it was the colour of silver but was liquid and so seemed to be alive or *quick*—the phrase *the quick and the dead* includes the same idea—and because it was widely used by doctors it's sometimes suggested that *quack* comes from *quicksilver*, but there's no connection.

Diseases and conditions

PHYSICIANS had an equally varied and often arcane vocabulary of words to describe the wide variety of diseases that they faced in everyday practice.

"Our castle's strength will laugh a siege to scorn," cried Macbeth in Shakespeare's Scottish play. "Here let them lie till famine and the ague eat them up." **Ague** was a general medical term for a condition that was once all too common in marshy or damp parts of Britain (Oliver Cromwell died of it in 1658), though neither the name nor the disease is encountered these days in Britain. It was a type of *malaria* (which comes from the Italian *mala aria*, bad air, because it was thought an unwholesome atmosphere or miasma carried the disease from boggy places).

At one time, Londoners suffered an annual epidemic of the fever that lasted from March to July. It was often called the **tertian ague**, because the fever recurred every other day (*tertian* is actually from the Latin word meaning "third", but the episodes were counted inclusively). The **bastard tertian** resembled a tertian ague but wasn't exactly the same thing. Another was the **quartan ague** (from Latin *quartus*, fourth) which recurred every third day; there was also the **quotidian ague** (Latin *quotidianus*, daily), in which the fever came every day. Shakespeare had some fun with common ignorance of these medical terms in *Henry V*, when Hostess Quickly spoke of Sir John Falstaff:

> Ah, poor heart! he is so shaked of a burning
> quotidian tertian, that it is most lamentable to
> behold.

"Quotidian tertian": daily, every third day? I don't think so. There were no known cures for these diseases, though some said that the magical incantation **abracadabra** (an extremely ancient word, probably from Aramaic or Hebrew) was efficacious against the tertian ague.

Shakespeare's characters often use phrases like "A pox on him!" and "A pox on't!" as terms of irritation. **Pox** by itself was a general term for any venereal disease, but doctors and lay people used the word for a whole set of diseases that all formed raised *pocks* or pustules on the skin. Examples survive in *chickenpox* and *smallpox* (though the latter has now thankfully been eradicated worldwide). **Water-pox**, **wind-pox**, and **swine-pox** were other names for chickenpox, while **cowpox** was a relatively benign occupational disease of milkmaids that they caught from the teats of cows; it protected them against smallpox, so it formed the basis of early vaccines. **Grease-pox** was caught from a disease of horses' hooves called the **grease**. The **French pox**, **great pox**, or **Spanish pox** were various terms for syphilis. A **pox-doctor** specialized in treating venereal diseases.

Another general term was **flux**, any abnormally copious flowing of blood or other matter from the body's organs. It was an old name for dysentery, for which other terms were **red flux** or **bloody flux**. This last term was used by Margaret Mitchell in *Gone with the Wind*:

> As for dysentery—the 'bloody flux' as the ladies delicately called it—it seemed to have spared no one from private to general.

A further set of names existed for another dangerous disease of people confined together for long periods. We call it typhus these days, but at one time it was more commonly known as **jail fever**, **hospital fever**, **ship fever**, or **camp fever**, among others.

Gout is a term that's unfortunately still well known, though we have less need now to refer to **saturnine gout**. This was an eighteenth-century term for a variety caused by drinking wine contaminated by lead; its name comes from the alchemists' association of the planet Saturn with that element. A related disease of the century was **Devonshire colic**, eventually identified as lead poisoning caused by acidic apple juice absorbing the metal from the lead linings of West Country cider presses. The following century saw **painter's colic**, caused by fumes from the lead-based paints of the period, which features in *The Diary of a Nobody* by George Grossmith:

> Woke up with a fearful headache and strong symptoms of a cold. Carrie, with a perversity which is just like her, said it was 'painter's colic,' and was the result of my having spent the last few days with my nose over a paint-pot.

There were once many such occupational diseases, such as **hatter's shakes**, caused by inhaling mercury vapour from the processing of felt; **brass founder's ague**, from zinc fumes; **gold-smelter's cataract**, an eye disease caused by staring at the bright molten metal; and **miner's asthma**, silicosis from inhaling rock dust. **Woolsorter's disease** was anthrax acquired from fleeces. There were many others identified in the nineteenth century, some of which sound humorous to us today, though they were serious enough for their sufferers: **dustman's shoulder**, **lighterman's bottom**, **nun's bursitis**, **potter's rot**, and **washerwoman's itch**.

Dropsy is an old-fashioned term for what doctors now call *oedema*, in which a watery fluid collects in the body (it comes in a complicated way via the older *idropesie* and *hydropsy* from the Greek *hudor*, water). Samuel Johnson suffered badly from it in later years and he wrote in sadness about it to James Boswell in February 1784:

> A dropsy gains ground upon me; my legs and thighs are very much swollen with water, which I should be content if I could keep there, but I am afraid that it will soon be higher.

The **king's evil** or **scrofula** was a form of tuberculosis in the glands of the neck. It was believed that the mere touch of the monarch could cure it. The latter name is from the Latin *scrofa*, a breeding sow, because these animals were thought to catch the disease. Samuel Pepys twice mentions observing the ceremony at which people suffering from the disease were brought to be cured:

> 23 June 1660. So to my Lord's lodgings, where Tom Guy came to me, and there staid to see the King touch people for the King's evil.

Those touched were given a coin called an *angel*, because of the picture stamped on one side. When angels stopped being coined—before Pepys's time—a medal called a **touch-piece** was provided instead.

One set of antique medical words end in *-thropy*, taken from the Greek *anthropos*, man. Some we still actively use, such as *philan-thropy*, an active effort to promote human welfare, *misanthropy*, a hatred or distrust of mankind, and *lycanthropy* (Greek *lykos*, wolf), becoming a werewolf, something once thought to be caused by witchcraft or magic. **Apanthropy**, as another example, means a love of solitude (it's from Greek *apān*, apart). Some that have vanished from the everyday lexicon refer to a man imagining himself to be some animal: **cynanthropy** or **kynanthropy** (Greek *kynos*, dog), **hippanthropy** (Greek *hippos*, horse), and the extremely rare **boanthropy** (Greek *bous*, ox), an allusion to what happened to Nebuchadnezzar in Chapter 4 of the book of Daniel, in which as a result of pride "he was driven from men, and did eat grass as oxen". The general term is **zoanthropy** (Greek *zōïon*, animal).

Another set of rare words, ending in *-mania*, are about madnesses of a specific sort. Lots of examples appear in present-day classifications of abnormal states and there are hundreds of others, some serious but mostly humorous, for an immoderate attraction, such as *balletomania*, a passionate addiction to ballet, or *infomania*, an excessive enthusiasm for accumulating factual information. Few of them are true medical disorders; for example, **potichomania** (French *potiche*, an oriental porcelain vase) was a nineteenth-century craze for imitating Japanese or other porcelain by covering the inner surface of glass vessels and the like with designs on paper or sheet gelatine. However, **arithromania** is an old term—once used by Freud—for an irresistible desire to count objects and make calculations, which today would be considered a case of obsessive compulsive disorder. **Sitiomania**

(Greek *sition*, food made from grain) was a morbid aversion to food, a condition that, with its sufferer, was likely to be short-lived. **Lypemania** (Greek *lupē*, grief) was a nineteenth-century term for extreme mournfulness that we would now describe as intense nervous depression.

Centuries ago, you might have described these as cases of **deliraments** (from Latin *delirare*, to be crazy, from *lira*, ridge or furrow; to the Romans a person who was mad wasn't out of his tree but out of his furrow, so off the straight and narrow; *delirium* and *delirious* share its origin). A **lunatic asylum** or **mad-house** (two terms now expunged from psychiatric terminology) was once called **Bedlam** and a madman had the generic name of **Jack O'Bedlam**. *Bedlam* was an abbreviated form of the name of the hospital of St Mary of Bethlehem, an ancient London-based refuge for mentally ill people. Because it was a noisy and chaotic place, the word has gone into the language to mean a scene of uproar and confusion. When Thomas Gray included the line "Far from the madding crowd's ignoble strife" in his *Elegy Written in a Country Churchyard*, he was using **madding** for madness or becoming mad, which survives only in set phrases like his.

PART 3

Entertainment
& Leisure

Games with cards

CARD GAMES have been popular entertainments for centuries. Every age has had its fashionable varieties, which anybody who wanted to be socially capable needed to learn.

These days, it's **bridge** (originally *biritch* in the middle nineteenth century, a mysterious name, though it's likely to be from the eastern Mediterranean, since a form of the game has long been known there). Before that the most prestigious game was **whist** (originally *whisk*, possibly because tricks are whisked away by the winner, though a writer in 1688 argued that it "is called Whist from the silence that is to be observed in the play" and Dr Johnson similarly defined the word in his *Dictionary* of 1755 as "a game at cards, requiring close attention and silence"; *whist* here is an obsolete forceful request for silence, as in *to hold one's whist*, to keep quiet). In the eighteenth century a form of whist was sometimes known as **swabbers**, from the name given to certain cards—the ace of hearts, the knave or jack of clubs, and the ace and deuce of trumps—though nobody knows why.

Whist is recorded for the first time in 1663, just after the restoration of the English monarchy. But at that time everyone with social aspirations wanted to play **ombre**, a game for three people that Charles II and his courtiers brought back with them from the continent. However, *ombre* was originally Spanish, and the name is a corruption of *hombre*, man, because the person who chose the trumps and sought to win the pool was "the man" (the name was usually said like "omber", though some said it as "ombray" to be nearer the original Spanish). It was popular for generations in Europe, so it has had many other names as well, among them **el tresillo** (from a Spanish word for a three-seat sofa, because of the three players), **rocambor** (in South America), **l'hombre**, and **mediator**. Ombre stayed in fashion into the early eighteenth century; its rules were a bit like those of the modern game of nap, though more complicated, and full of strange foreign terms: *Codillio, Repuesto, Voll, Gagno, Basto.* The person who lost a hand was said to be *beasted* (why is hard to understand) and so an early alternative name was **beast**. It was immortalized in Alexander Pope's poem *The Rape of the Lock* of 1714, in which a game is described in detail, though in terms that are incomprehensible to us today without a lot of footnotes:

> The skilful Nymph reviews her force with care:
> Let Spades be trumps! she said, and trumps they
> were.
> Now move to war her sable Matadores,
> In show like leaders of the swarthy Moors.

> Spadillio first, unconquerable Lord!
> Led off two captive trumps, and swept the board.
> As many more Manillio forc'd to yield,
> And march'd a victor from the verdant field.

The *matadores* were the highest-ranking cards in the deck; *spadillio* was the ace of spades and *manillio* the two of spades; the *verdant field* was the green baize surface of the card table.

Another game Charles II's court brought over was **basset**, whose name derives from an Italian word (it's first recorded being played in Venice) meaning something base or low. This was a gambling game in which players played against a dealer or banker; it had a reputation for high stakes and the risk of winning or losing large sums of money. John Evelyn recorded in his diary in February 1685 that he had found Charles II and several people of rank playing basset with a bank of at least £2,000 in gold, worth more than £150,000 today. It is notable as being the first game in which *punter* was used to describe one of the players against the bank; this came from the verb *to punt* with related sense, though unfortunately we don't know where that comes from. Around the 1730s basset became known as **pharaoh**; it was often said, without much evidence, that the name derived from the picture on the king of hearts in packs of cards imported from France. It travelled to the US, where it was known as **faro** (said the same way) and became a popular gambling game in the nineteenth century, for example on Mississippi riverboats.

Yet another Restoration import was **loo**, nothing to do with the twentieth-century slang term for a lavatory, but an abbreviation of **lanterloo**, from the meaningless French word *lenturlu* that appeared in seventeenth-century lullabies. This was an even more disreputable gambling game, because the pot could quickly grow to very large sizes and bankrupt unwary players. A less dangerous version could be played at home and appears in the novels of Jane Austen, as here in *Pride and Prejudice* (1796):

> On entering the drawing-room she found the whole party at loo, and was immediately invited to join them; but suspecting them to be playing high, she declined it.

As an etymological aside, the jack of clubs in loo—the highest trump—had the nickname *Pam*; this had been abbreviated from Latin *Pamphilus* (derived from Greek *pamphilos*, beloved by all), in turn from the title of a famous twelfth-century Latin love poem, *Pamphilus, seu de Amore* ("Pamphilus, or about Love"), which is also the origin of our *pamphlet*.

Ombre was deposed in the eighteenth century by **quadrille** (nothing to do with the dance of the same name, though its influence—in French—caused the name to change from the Spanish *cuartillo*, from *cuarto*, fourth, because the game was for four players). This was a development of ombre that became a widely played game in France for about a century. In England, though, its pre-eminence was comparatively brief, since it lost out to whist. This was largely because quadrille was complicated, made more so by the order of the cards in two of the suits being back to front, so that the lowest numbered cards had the highest value.

These card games fashionable after the Restoration replaced others popular before the English Civil War. One, reputedly of Gaelic origin and known in both Ireland and Scotland, was **maw** (a name of obscure origin), which is an ancestor of the modern Irish game **twenty-five** (because that's the winning score). This was James VI's favourite game; it was brought south on his accession as James I of England in 1603 and was for some decades the most popular game at the English court. However, the king's card-playing skills left much to be desired according to William Chatto, a historian of card games, who observed two centuries later that:

> His Majesty appears to have played at cards just as he played with affairs of State—in an indolent manner, requiring in both cases someone to hold his cards, if not to prompt him what to play.

The game came back into popularity in the nineteenth century under the name **spoil-five** (because the game is said to be *spoiled* if no player wins three out of a possible five tricks) and sometimes **jink**, which for some reason was the name given to winning all five tricks.

Such courtly fashion hardly affected the popularity of games played by the ordinary people and known from previous centuries. Among them was **bone-ace**, first recorded in 1611 and an ancestor to blackjack, in which the third card dealt to each player was turned up, and the player who had the highest obtained the *bone* or half the stake. **Gleek** (possibly from Middle Dutch *ghelic*, like, since the possession of three cards of the same kind—called a *gleek*—was a feature of the game) is known from the sixteenth century, though it wasn't described in detail until 1662; it's a sort of ancestor of piquet.

Primero is a Spanish gambling game, especially popular from about 1530 to 1640, that is one of the ancestors of poker. In *Henry VIII* Shakespeare has the king playing it on the night Queen Elizabeth was born:

> LOVELL. Came you from the King, my lord?
> GARDINER. I did, Sir Thomas; and left him at
> primero With the Duke of Suffolk.

It developed into **brag**, whose name is from the *brag* or challenge given by one of the players to the rest to turn up cards equal in value to his, which was also known as **pocher** (German *pochen*, to boast) from which the name of *poker* probably derives.

There are hundreds of other card games that have been invented at various times, most of whose names have meanings lost in time. Some others of the sixteenth century are **laugh and lay** down, **loadum** (which might at first have been *load 'em* because a similar game was called in Italian *carica l'asino*, load the ass), **mack**, **noddy** (a direct ancestor of cribbage, played on a **noddy-board**), and **trump** (also known as **ruff** and **honours**). The seventeenth century had **angel-beast** (in which the *angel* was the stake) and **cornet**.

In the early eighteenth century **all fours** was first recorded, named in part because it was a game for four players but also because there were four scoring chances, called *high*, *low*, *Jack*, and *game*; it was later taken to America where it has variously been called **seven-up** (because a score of seven points wins the game), **old sledge**, **pitch**, **setback**, or **cinch**. This remained popular through the following century in Britain and is mentioned in Charles Dickens's *Pickwick Papers*:

> Four or five great hulking fellows, just visible through a cloud of tobacco smoke, were engaged in noisy and riotous conversation over half-emptied pots of beer, or playing at all-fours with a very greasy pack of cards.

Later in the eighteenth century **reversis** was imported from France. It was called that because—like **hearts**, of which it's an ancestor—the idea was to avoid taking tricks or acquiring certain penalty cards, the reverse of most games.

A popular game of the nineteenth century, though its name had been first recorded a century earlier, was **Pope Joan**, named for some inexplicable reason after the fictional female pope of the ninth century (the French name for it was *nain jaune*, the yellow dwarf, and it's just possible the English name is a corruption of it via some such form as *nun joan*). This later developed into the modern *Newmarket* (*Michigan* in the United States) and is very similar to another called **matrimony**.

One that's especially obscure is the nineteenth-century game of **able-whackets**, which was described by Admiral William Smyth in his *Sailor's Word-book* of 1865 as

> A popular sea-game with cards, wherein the loser is beaten over the palms of the hands with a handkerchief tightly twisted like a rope. Very popular with horny-fisted sailors.

No other details are known.

Games with things

THOUGH CARD GAMES were popular, they were often the province of older men and women. Younger ones usually preferred something more active.

In 1621, Robert Burton wrote in *The Anatomy of Melancholy*:

> The ordinary recreations which we have in winter,
> and in most solitary times busy our minds with,
> are cards, tables and dice, shovelboard, chess-
> play, the philosopher's game, small trunks,
> shuttlecock, billiards, music, masks, singing,
> dancing ....

He considered melancholy to be innate in humankind, and to avoid it he advised, "Be not solitary, be not idle." On those long winter days when other occupations were unavailable, games and amusements in company with others fitted his recommendation to a T.

Some of them are familiar to us, such as **chess** (from Old French *esches*, plural of *eschec*, a check). One that may seem to be but is misleading is **billiards**, of which more later. The children's game of **shuttlecock** is more fully called **battledore and shuttlecock**; the *battledore* is the bat, whose name may be from Provençal *batedor*, beater, because the name was given to the similar tool once used to beat clothes in a washtub (*beater* has been reintroduced in J K Rowling's *Harry Potter* books for a team member in Quidditch); the *shuttlecock* is the feathery ball that is also used in badminton, the game's grown-up successor; it seems to have been called that because at first it was made of chicken (or cock) feathers stuck in a cork and because it *shuttles* back and forth. **Tables** is the old name for what later in the seventeenth century started to be called **backgammon** (from Old English *gamen*, a game, with *back* prefixed because, the experts guess, pieces sometimes have to go back and re-enter the table again); the older name may have been the origin of the expression *to turn the tables* on your opponent, because of the sudden reversals of fortune that can occur. **Mask** here is the then common English spelling of **masque**—we've since settled on the French original—a dramatic entertainment that was popular in the royal court and among the nobility in sixteenth- and seventeenth-century England, which consisted of dancing and acting by players in masks. It developed in part out of older **guisings** (from the same root as *disguise*), in which a masked allegorical figure would appear and address the assembled company.

The one that may be least familiar is the **philosopher's game**. This is a very old pastime, known from the eleventh century. It has had many other names, such as **Arithmomachia**, **Rythmomachia**, and **Rhythmomachy**; all derive from Greek *makhē*, battle, and the last two also feature *rythmos*, arithmetic (it was also known as **ludus philosophorum**, which is just the Latin for philosopher's game). In Burton's time it was played on a double-sized chessboard (16 squares by eight), with triangles, squares, circles, and pyramids as pieces, all with number values on them—one of its oddities was that the number values weren't the same for both players. Its rules were complicated, and read like a mathematical version of chess; for example, you could capture an enemy piece by moving two of your own to either side of it, provided that the values of your pieces added up to the value of the enemy piece. It was once extremely popular, but lost out to chess in the sixteenth century, though it has been rediscovered in very recent times.

Shovelboard was another name for what we would now call **shove-halfpenny**, a classic pub game, which has also been called **slide-thrift**, **slidegroat**, **slip-groat**, or **shove-groat** (a *groat* is an old coin worth fourpence, or a little over 1½ modern pence, though by Shakespeare's time the coin that was sometimes mentioned was a silver shilling, equivalent to 5p now but much more valuable then). In all these games a coin is propelled up a smooth table by the edge of the hand, with the aim being to get it to stop between lines ruled across the table. Burton's name of **shovel-board** was later borrowed for a different pastime, the one-time classic shipboard game that more recently still has become known as **shuffleboard**.

Trunks is one name for a game that was at one time played on a bench with eleven numbered holes pierced at one end, into which small bowls had to be rolled. The game was commonly called **troll-madam** or **trou-madame** (*troll* is a misunderstanding or mishearing by English people of French *trou*, hole), and by those names is recorded from the sixteenth century as being played especially by women. It seems to have gone under other aliases as well, since contemporary records also call it **trucks** and **pigeon-holes**; it also had widely varying types of board and numbers of holes. Under the name of *trou-madame* it survived into the twentieth century, though by then it had long been played on a table like a long, thin billiards table with a set of holes at the far end, the balls being hit with a cue; this was similar to the original form of **bagatelle**. This is a French word borrowed from the Italian *bagatella*, perhaps from *baga* in the sense of baggage, or from a diminutive of Latin *baca*, berry; our expression *mere bagatelle* for something too unimportant or easy to be worth bothering with seems to come from the game, an illustration of how little skill it was thought to require. Another version recorded in the 1850s was called **cockamaroo** or **Russian bagatelle**, though this does seem to have been more complicated: the 1911 edition of the *Encyclopaedia Britannica* says it was played on a table

> prepared with a number of pins, holes, arches, and bells, up to and through which the ball is played from the baulk end of the table. It is a childish amusement, requiring little skill.

Burton doesn't mention **skittles**, but it has been a traditional game for as far back as records exist, often under the name of **ninepins**; it survives as a pub game, sometimes in the form of **table skittles**, in which the pins have to be knocked down by a ball on a suspended string. One reference, in Joseph Strutt's *Sports and Pastimes* of 1801, says that a game called **bubble the justice** had been invented to defeat a law that prohibited skittles because people gambled on it; its odd name is from contemporary slang: to *bubble* was to deceive, so it meant "cheat the magistrate". One version of skittles has fallen completely out of memory. It was called variously **half-bowl** or **roly-poly** and is first recorded in an Act of Parliament of 1477-78. This was a miniature form of skittles, with either 12 or 15 pins arranged in a two-foot circle. The big difference to other skilled games was that the ball was half a sphere (hence *half-bowl*), so making it difficult to send it where you wanted it.

Burton doesn't mention any gambling game, but the one gamblers preferred in his time and for centuries before was called **hazard**, a dice game in which one's chances of winning were controlled by complicated and arbitrary rules. The name is recorded from about 1300; its name came through Old French and Spanish from Arabic *az-zahr*, chance or luck, which in turn is from Persian *zār* or Turkish *zar*, dice. The game was so hard to play well, with such traps for the unwary player, that *hazard* later turned into a figurative term for peril or jeopardy. Much later still hazard formed the basis of the American game of **craps** (possibly from **crab**, the eighteenth-century slang term for the lowest throw at hazard of two ones, perhaps in turn from *crab's eyes* for the two spots). Hazard was considered to be so great a danger to the well-being of the public that it was banned in Britain in 1738.

A dice game of the nineteenth century was called **grand hazard**, but it had little to do with the older one, employing three dice rather than the two of hazard and needing a complex semicircular layout like half a roulette table, with options for betting on odds or evens or other combinations. The dice were usually spun in a wire contraption called a **birdcage**. A simpler version in North America was called **chuck-a-luck**; it used a horn-shaped chute which contained a set of inclined planes to tumble the dice as they fell, and a flat area on which the dice fell and whose layout decided whether the player had won or not; this was much simpler than grand hazard, consisting only of six areas. Chuck-a-luck was unsophisticated and easy to set up, so it was the province of small-time gamblers on riverboats, on street corners, or in low gaming establishments. Though the proper horn was of leather, those with limited resources used a cruder one made of tin; an operator like this came to be called a **tinhorn gambler** or just a **tinhorn**, at first a derogatory term for a cheap gambler, but more recently anybody who pretends to have money, ability, or influence.

Outdoor games

WHEN THE WEATHER was suitable, other games were played that needed a larger space than any house could provide.

Samuel Pepys wrote in his diary for 2 April 1661:

> So I into St. James's Park, where I saw the Duke of York playing at Pelemele, the first time that ever I saw the sport.

Its name was more usually spelled **pall-mall**, but he no doubt wrote it as he heard it in upper-class speech. He saw it played where London's Pall Mall now runs (the game was the direct origin of the street name) but the course was shifted later that same year, it is said because dust from royal carriages disrupted games. The new course was about 800 yards long, laid out where The Mall now lies. Pall-mall seems to have been a weird cross between croquet and golf, using a mallet and a boxwood ball a foot in diameter. The players drove the ball along the course by taking immense swings at it with the mallet. To end the game they then had to shoot the ball through a suspended hoop at one end. The person who required the fewest shots won. The name actually means "ball and mallet" and comes via the obsolete French *pallemaille* from Italian *pallamaglio* (*palla*, ball + *maglio*, mallet).

A much older game, called **loggats** or **loggets** (probably a variant of *log*), was a traditional country recreation. You threw heavy sticks about two feet in length (the *loggats*) at a fixed mark, often a post, and the person who got nearest to it won. This explains an otherwise puzzling reference in Shakespeare's *Hamlet*:

> Did these bones cost no more the breeding but to
> play at loggets with 'em?

Another game was even older, a poorly recorded one called **closh**. The name comes from the Dutch word *klos* for a wooden ball or bowl and it seems to have been a Dutch import in the fifteenth century. The bowl had to be driven through a hoop or ring, as in croquet, by a spade-shaped mallet that the Dutch called a *klos-beytel* (the second part is related to our *beetle*, for a heavy mallet, as in *beetle and wedge*, a once-common pair of tools for splitting timber into firewood—now best known as the name of some English pubs). Games such as closh, skittles, and bowls were much looked down on by the authorities at one time and there are several acts of Parliament of the sixteenth century forbidding them.

Yet another early game, which some writers have called **ground**

billiards, might be no more than a variation on closh. It was played on a small outdoor court with a hoop at one end and an upright stick at the other, with balls hit by a mallet. There's some evidence that it was played for several centuries from about 1300 onwards. The name *ground billiards* has been given to it because it was brought indoors about 1600 and turned into a table game that is the ancestor of our modern **billiards** (whose name, by the way, is from French *billard*, used both for the game and for the cue, derived from *bille*, a billet of wood). This indoor version copied the layout of the outdoor game, with a croquet-like hoop at one end called the **pass** or **port** and a skittle at the other called the **king**, both set on a green baize cloth that may have been intended to remind players of the lawn in the outdoor game. The cues were called **maces** and illustrations of the seventeenth century show them to have curved ends like small hockey sticks, nothing like the cues that were adopted later.

In the nineteenth century, a game called **lawn billiards**, or **troco**, was played in English gardens. That invaluable Victorian guide to every necessity of domestic life, *Enquire Within Upon Everything* (which by 1900 had reached its 90th edition with sales of well over a million copies), described it under both names:

> In the centre of the Troco ground is fixed a ring of iron, which moves freely on a pivot, the spike of the ring being driven into a piece of wood let into the ground. The wooden ball is lifted from the

> ground by means of the spoon-ended cue,
> and thrown towards the ring—the object of
> the player being to pass the ball through the
> ring.

There's a peculiarity about the history of the name *troco* (altered from Italian *trucco* for a billiard table), as it was described in 1598 by John Florio, the British-born son of an Italian refugee, as a table game, a sort of indoor skittles, but then the word seems to vanish again until the nineteenth century.

Going back to late medieval times, an early game that might be an ancestor of both cricket and baseball was being played by country girls; it was called **stoolball**, just possibly because the wicket was originally a stool, though later illustrations show it to be a square wooden panel fixed to a pole at about chest height. The batsman (always so called even though most were female) was armed with an implement that looks like a large table-tennis bat, made of willow. Andrew Lang, in his book on Oxford dated 1882, wrote:

> A young man's fancy lightly turns to the
> Beaumont, north of the modern Beaumont
> Street, where there are wide playing-fields, and
> space for archery, foot-ball, stool-ball, and other
> sports.

The game died out in the late nineteenth century in most places but it is still played in Sussex.

Confusingly, there was another game, variously called **stow-ball**, **stopball**, **stoball**, or **stobball** (whose name may be from *stob*, a stake or post, which might have been the club or staff involved), that some writers believe is the same as stoolball. But John Aubrey described the game in his *Natural History of Wiltshire*, written about 1686:

> They smite a ball, stuffed very hard with quills and covered with sole leather, with a staff, commonly made of withy, about three feet and a half long… A stobball-ball is of about four inches diameter, and as hard as a stone.

If we ignore the size and nature of the ball, this sounds a bit like golf. But from that description, it might just as well have been an early form of hockey that was also known as **bandy-ball** or **bandy** (a word that once meant to pass a ball to and fro in various games, which may be from French *bander*, to take sides at tennis; it's the origin of *to bandy about*).

Another traditional country game was called **barley break**. This was played on any suitable patch of ground and might have got its name because it was played at harvest time among the stooks of barley. The playing area was divided into three parts, of which the middle one was called **hell**. It was played by three men and three women hand-in-hand in couples. One couple stood in the middle area and tried to catch the other two couples, who were allowed to separate or *break* when at risk of being captured. If one of them was caught, the couple had to take their turn in the middle; the object was to be the last couple caught. This game gave rise to a saying, **the last couple in hell**, which turns up in the 1610 play, *The Scornful Lady*, by Francis Beaumont and John Fletcher and also explains the reference in one of Robert Herrick's poems, *Barley-Break, or Last in Hell*:

> We two are last in hell; what may we fear
> To be tormented or kept pris'ners here?
> Alas! if kissing be of plagues the worst,
> We'll wish in hell we had been last and first.

Invitation to a dance

BACK INDOORS, another active pursuit was dancing. Jane Austen was a passionate dancer and her novels lead us into the language of the pastime.

In *Pride and Prejudice*, Jane Austen remarks that "To be fond of dancing was a certain step towards falling in love" and most of her heroines either met their lovers at a dance, or a ball was a key scene in the development of a romance.

From an etymological point of view, it's therefore intriguing to note how few names of dances she mentions. In her early novel *Love and Friendship* Laura comments in passing that she has forgotten the steps for the **minuet**; in *Mansfield Park* Tom Bertram demands a play with "a figure-dance, and a hornpipe, and a song between the acts". The most common reference is to a **country dance**. In *Northanger Abbey* Mr Tilney says, "I consider a country-dance as an emblem of marriage."

They were called *country dances* because they were the everyday dances of the people of the country (England, that is, not necessarily because they were rural). The term had been taken over to France—almost a century before her time—and was converted by mistake to *contre-danse*. This was because these imported country dances involved longways sets, with a row of men and women standing opposite each other and in which each couple in turn danced its way between the lines to its head; so *contra-* or *contre-*, opposite. When new French dances developed from them were brought back into England, their name was Anglicized as **contra-dances**; some people thought this was the correct term and that *country dance* was an ignorant error. Such are the subtleties and confusions of word history.

One dance of this sort brought over from France was the **quadrille** (from the Italian *quadriglia* for a small company of cavalry, from *quadra*, a square), which in 1865 Lewis Carroll was to gently mock with his absurd lobster quadrille in *Alice in Wonderland*. Miss Austen does not notice it—for her, quadrille was a card game, played by senior members of an assembly as an alternative to dancing; in any case the dance only really became fashionable after her death in 1817. It was a type of square dance, requiring four couples, and danced in five sections called **figures** (because of the step patterns in the diagrams supplied in manuals of dancing), each of which was a dance in itself. There were hundreds of combinations of steps possible and whole books were devoted to describing them. Its French origin is very clear from the names of the individual parts, all based on names for older French dances: *Le pantalon*, *L'été*, *La poule*, either *La pastourelle* or *La trénise* (sometimes both), and *Le final*.

What she does mention, however, is the **cotillion** (a *cotillon* was a French peasant girl's petticoat; the word became attached to the dance because it was common for young women taking part to pin up their long skirts, so making their petticoats visible; another name was **contredanse française**). This was a precursor of the quadrille that had come over from France about 1770 and often began an evening's entertainment. The cotillion required four couples in a square, dancing various figures, which in later years could be quite intricate. In the US, *cotillion* became the usual term for a quadrille and remains a common name for a formal ball. In the 1840s a variant called the **German cotillion**, in which the dancers moved with arms interlaced in the German style, often ended an evening's dancing. This became popular in North America as **The German**; an article in *The Galaxy* of New York in 1867 explained,

> The figures of 'The German' generally open with a grouping of a certain number of couples, who pass and re-pass, turn or bow, as in an ordinary cotillion, performing a routine of movement, directed by the leader, and at the conclusion of which the galop or waltz is taken up and danced for a few bars, when the dancers retire to their

> seats, technically called 'home,' to give place to
> other couples, who execute the same
> manoeuvres.

That description includes names for two of the dances that superseded the ones Jane Austen loved. The **galop** (the French for "gallop", whose name had come into English in the 1830s) was a lively dance in 2/4 time, described as "the quintessence of all fast dances" by one contemporary, which also often formed one part of the quadrille. The **waltz** (German *walzen*, to roll or revolve), is too familiar still to need much comment, though the *Times* of 16 July 1816 fulminated against it, following its introduction at court only the week before:

> It is quite sufficient to cast one's eyes on the
> voluptuous intertwining of the limbs, and close
> compressure of the bodies, in this dance, to see
> that it is far indeed removed from the modest
> reserve which has hitherto been considered
> distinctive of English females. So long as this
> obscene display was confined to prostitutes and
> adulteresses, we did not think it deserving of
> notice, but now that it is attempted to be forced
> on the respectable classes of society by the evil
> example of their superiors, we feel it a duty to
> warn every parent against exposing his daughter
> to so fatal a contagion.

A polemical article on the freedom of women to engage in such modern dances in *Puttnam's Magazine* in 1853 said:

> The day, thank Heaven, has come, when every
> woman may waltz and polk, and join to her heart's
> content in the healthful redowa, mazurka, or the
> new Russian dance—honest diversions, which
> unite exercise and amusement.

We don't use the vaguely rude-sounding verb **polk** any more,
though she clearly means dancing the **polka**, a Bohemian dance
whose name is from either Czech *půlka*, a half-step, or Czech
polka, a Polish woman (opinions differ), and which became a
craze for a while after it was introduced to London in 1844. The
redowa was another Bohemian dance, in 3/4 time, whose name
is also Czech, from *rej*, a round dance. The **mazurka** was Polish
(from *mazurka*, a woman of the Mazovia province of that
country).

Others the writer might have mentioned were the **varsovienne**
or **varsoviana** (from French *Varsovie*, Warsaw), a genteel variation on the mazurka; another Polish dance, the **krakowiak** or
Cracovienne (from the Polish city *Kraków* or *Cracow*); the **schot-
tische**, a slow polka whose name comes from German *der schot-
tische Tanz*, the Scottish dance—though it has little to do with
Scotland—in which the polka step was enlivened with a circular
hop (in the 1880s the popularity of Tom Turner's *Dancing in the
Barn Schottisch* from the US caused a variant to become known as
the **barn dance**); and the **lancers**, originally called *quadrille des
lanciers* (**quadrille of the lancers**), for eight or sixteen pairs,

supposedly based on a military dance using lances and which had been introduced from Paris in 1836. Older British readers will remember Mr Pastry, Richard Hearne, who had an act in which he danced the lancers—by himself—with more enthusiasm than skill, progressively getting out of time with his invisible partners. It would mean little to an audience today, who would have even less idea what was going on than those of the 1950s.

Dancing manuals of the middle of the nineteenth century mention the **zingerilla**, the **zulma l'orientale**, the **Sicilienne**, and the **Esmeralda**, the source of whose names can sometimes only be guessed at. Hardly any of these made a noticeable splash. Another was the **gorlitza** (a Polish round dance for two, named after the place now called *Gorlice*, introduced to London from Paris in 1851), of which George Routledge wrote in his *Manual of Etiquette* in 1875:

> Like the Varsovienne, it is now seldom seen
> beyond the walls of the dancing academy.
> Perhaps one reason of its short-lived popularity is
> to be found in the fact that it is rather
> troublesome to learn, the steps being changed
> continually.

Formal balls of this period often started with a **polonaise**. The *Daily Telegraph* reported of a German example in 1861:

> The ball ... commenced with a sort of general
> perambulation in couples. It is not dancing, ... it

> is simply walking to the music. This solemn
> promenade is known as a Polonaise.

It was a dignified ceremonial, a processional rather than a dance in the ordinary sense, which opened very formal balls.

Long before Jane Austen's time, at the Restoration of Charles II, dances of different sorts were fashionable. One was the **branle** or **bransle** (from French *branler*, to shake, for no clear reason), mentioned by Pepys in a description of a royal ball he attended at Whitehall on 31 December 1662:

> By-and-by comes the king and queene, the duke
> and duchess, and all the great ones; and, after
> seating themselves, the king takes out the
> Duchess of York; and the duke the Duchess of
> Buckingham; the Duke of Monmouth my Lady
> Castlemaine; and so other lords other ladies; and
> they danced the bransle.

Earlier, this had been known as the **braule** or **brawl** (Shakespeare has it in *Love's Labour's Lost*: "Will you win your love with a French braule?"), but that was just a variation on the French name and nothing to do with a noisy quarrel; the **caterbrawl**, which sounds like a cat fight, was a type for four couples (*cater* is from French *quatre*, four).

Pepys goes on to say, "After that, the king led a lady a single **coranto**." The French original, *courante*, literally meant a running dance, one with a running or gliding step rather than a leap;

courante or variations on it were common—in *Henry V*, Shakespeare has Britaine, one of the Advisors to the King of France, say:

> They bid us to the English Dancing-Schools, And
> teach Lavoltas high, and swift Carrantos.

The **lavolta** was also called the **volte** or **volta**, taken from its name in French and Italian and meaning a turn. It was a lively dance for a couple in which at one point the woman springs into the air in the happy expectation of being caught by her partner. The **sarabande** is another couple dance in triple time of the same period that had evolved from the *zarabanda*, a Spanish dance of Latin America that had been banned in Spain in 1583 because it was considered to be obscene.

The lavolta opened with a **galliard**, another dance known to Shakespeare: in *Twelfth Night*, Sir Toby Belch asks Sir Andrew Aguecheek, "What is thy excellence in a galliard, knight?" which is the excuse for a bit of comic byplay that must have had them rolling in the aisles in Southwark. It was a show-off dance for expert male performers, involving complex jumps and changes of step, so determinedly masculine that some early descriptions had no female steps for it at all. The word first meant "valiant" or "sturdy" and later "lively and brisk"; it comes from an Old French word of Celtic origin. Closely associated with the galliard in Elizabethan times (though it had rather gone out by the Restoration) was the **pavan** or **pavane**, always described as slow and stately, one in which the performers were elaborately dressed, too much so for leaping about (you wouldn't think it, but the name is actually from the Italian city of *Padua*, via its dialect name *pavana*, filtered through French before reaching English). Another dance linked to the pavane was the **saltarello** (based on Latin *saltare*, to dance), which involved a lot of sudden skips and jumps for the couple.

Between the time of Pepys and Charles II and that of Jane Austen, many of these formal old dances drifted out of fashion to be replaced by others. The best known is the **minuet**, the one whose steps Laura (from *Love and Friendship*) had forgotten, and which by her time was going out of fashion again. It was another slow and stately ballroom dance for two in triple time, whose name came from French *menuet*, fine or delicate. The **gavotte** was somewhat similar; etymologically speaking this was the dance of the Gavots, a name that had been given in Provence to the natives of the Alps. There was also the **boree** or **bourrée**, another lively dance, whose name is from French *bourrée*, a country dance of the Auvergne.

Alongside such dances, participants would certainly have taken part in some of the progressive longways ones that Jane Austen knew, such as the **alman** or **almain** (a corruption of Old French *aleman*, German, that was a common general term at the time);

the **almain-leap** was one of its characteristic steps. In later years it became the **allemande**, though that could in the eighteenth century also be a figure dance (and nowadays it's a name in country dancing for a type of turn). Or they might have danced the **hey** (nobody seems to know where this came from), in which the women wound in and around their partners, in a foretaste of the reel. Of a different kind was the **hornpipe** that Tom Bertram (from *Mansfield Park*) pressed for, often a sailors' dance because it could be performed solo in all-male company, though on land the name could mean any dance performed to the musical in-strument of that name and could instead be a **jig** (or **gigue**) or a **reel**.

The food of love

MUSIC, not just for dancing but as an accompaniment to many parts of life, often used instruments
that are now almost unknown except to specialists.

In *The Fortunes of Nigel* of 1822, Sir Walter Scott described a Fleet
Street barber's shop:

> Within was the well-worn leather chair for
> customers, the guitar, then called a ghittern or
> cittern, with which a customer might amuse
> himself till his predecessor was dismissed from
> under Benjamin's hands, and which, therefore,
> often flayed the ears of the patient
> metaphorically, while his chin sustained from the
> razor literal scarification.

It was traditional for a person waiting to be shaved to entertain
the company with the instrument. The views of the barber, so
constantly exposed to frequently execrable musicianship, do not
seem to have been recorded, though Samuel Pepys disparagingly
called it **barber's music** (nothing at all to do with *barbershop music*,
a very different kind of music, from another country in a

different period). The **cittern** (or **cithern**, or **gittern**, all from the Greek *kithara* for an ancient stringed instrument) was certainly like a small version of the guitar whose name comes from the same source—though with brass strings rather than gut, and a lot more of them—but often had an elaborately wrought and grotesque head. A Tyrolean form later became popular as the **zither**. In the sixteenth century, the Greek word was probably borrowed a second time as **kit**, for a small fiddle popular with dancing masters because it was easy to carry about; however, the name might have been a joke, since its bigger relatives were strung with catgut, so making the little instruments *kittens*.

In John Rastell's play of about 1517, *The Interlude of the Four Elements*, a character says:

> This dance would do much better yet
> If we had a kit or taberet.

The **taberet**, or **tabaret** or **tabret**, was a drum. It's mentioned several times in the 1611 King James Bible, here in 1 Samuel, Chapter 10:

> Thou shalt meet a company of prophets coming
> down from the high place with a psaltery, and a
> tabret, and a pipe, and a harp, before them; and
> they shall prophesy.

It was a smaller version of the **tabor** (from Old French *tabour*, drum, which may be related to the Persian word for a drum, *tabra*; related words include **tambour**, another small drum, **tambourine**, and also the Indian **tabla**). The **pipe and tabor**, playable by one person, was an accompaniment to dances down to the seventeenth century and even later. It features in *The Life and Adventures of Sir Launcelot Greaves*, by Tobias Smollett (1762):

> The children welcomed him with their shrill
> shouts, the damsels with songs of praise, and the
> young men, with the pipe and tabor, marched
> before him to the May-pole, which was bedecked
> with flowers and bloom.

Francis Bacon mentions the cittern in his *Sylva* of 1626

> [The Irish harp] maketh a more Resounding
> Sound than a Bandora, Orpharion or Cittern,
> which have likewise Wire strings

and in fact there was a whole class of such plucked, wire-strung instruments. The **bandora** was the bass instrument of the family, also called the **bandore** or **pandora**. Its name goes back to Greek *pandoura*, an instrument supposedly invented by the god *Pan*; its name is confusingly like *pandōra*, which meant "all-gifted" and which was the name of the first mortal woman, who let out the evils of the world from *Pandora's Box*. The name was modified by Italians into **mandolin** and **mandola**, the latter being its larger relative; in the eighteenth century West Indian slaves turned *bandore* into **banjo**. The kitchen slicer called a **mandoline** is also from the same source, as is a rare adjective **panduriform**, which means fiddle-shaped.

The cittern, bandora, and **lute** (whose name is ultimately from Arabic *al-ūd*, preserved in the name of the *oud*, the modern lute of the Middle East) were three of the six instruments in the **English Consort**, the mainstay of the Elizabethan theatre and other entertainments, whose sound would often waft down unseen from a curtained gallery. One entertained the queen at the Earl of Hertford's Hampshire estate of Elvetham in 1591:

> After this speech, the Fairy Queen and her maids
> danced about the garland, singing a song of six
> partes, with the musicke of an exquisite consort,
> wherein was the Lute, Bandora, Base-Viol,
> Citterne, Treble-viol, and Flute.

Viol was a general name for a multi-stringed instrument played with a bow, which came through Old French *viele* from Provençal *viola*; our modern words **violin** and **viola** derive from its Italian relatives.

The **orpharion** that Bacon also mentions was supposedly a blend of *Orpheus* and *Arion*, those mythical musicians of antiquity. Unlike the bandora, it was a solo instrument, and one of considerable popularity, to judge from the number of times its name appeared in household inventories of the seventeenth century. There were many other stringed instruments, such as the **theorbo** (from Italian *tiorba*, though nobody knows where that comes from), a bass lute with two necks; the **chitarrone** (another Italian word, based on *chitarra*, guitar), which was a big theorbo; the **poliphant** or **polyphone** (Green *polyphanos*, having many tones), which Queen Elizabeth I liked to play; the **barbiton** (a Greek name); the **dyphone**, the double-lute that was invented by Thomas Mace in 1672; and the **sambuke** or **sambuka**, a triangular medieval instrument with a very shrill tone (its name comes from Greek *sambuke* for the elder tree from whose wood the instrument was supposedly made and which gave its name to the genus of the elder, *Sambucus*).

The **psaltery** is another ancient instrument mentioned in several places in the Bible (from Greek *psaltrion*, stringed instrument, which through Latin has also supplied us with *psalter*, a copy of the book of Psalms; *psalm* is from the related Greek *psalmos*, a song sung to harp music). Its appearances include—appropriately enough—Psalms Chapter 33:

> Praise the Lord with harp: sing unto him with the
> psaltery.

In shape it was rather like the **dulcimer** (whose name is probably from Latin *dulce melos*, sweet melody), though its strings were plucked, while those of the dulcimer are hit with little hammers. This, too, turns up in the King James Bible of 1611, in Chapter 3 of Daniel:

> Then an herald cried aloud, To you it is
> commanded, O people, nations, and languages,
> That at what time ye hear the sound of the cornet,
> flute, harp, sackbut, psaltery, dulcimer, and all
> kinds of musick, ye fall down and worship the
> golden image that Nebuchadnezzar the king hath
> set up.

Sackbut here is a mistranslation for *sambuka*, so it gives us the wrong idea completely. The medieval sackbut was a brass wind instrument, a predecessor of the trombone, whose name comes from the Old French *saqueboute*, a hook for pulling a man off a horse. An earlier translator of the Bible, Miles Coverdale, equally incorrectly used **shawm** instead. This was a double-reeded woodwind instrument, the forerunner of the oboe, which derives from the Old French *chalemel*, via Latin from Greek *kalamos*, reed. The *oboe*, though, was originally **hautboy** (from Old French *haut*, high + *bois*, wood). Falstaff in the second part of Shakespeare's *Henry IV* was very rude about the diminutive Justice Shallow, claiming that when naked he looked like a forked radish and that "the case of a treble hautboy was a mansion for him".

Edmund Spenser wrote in the *Faerie Queene* (1590),

> And after to his palace he them brings,
> With shawms, and trumpets, and with clarions
> sweet.

We may today be urged to action with clichéd *clarion cries* and even know of fictional newspapers called *The Clarion*, but the true and original **clarion** (from Latin *clarus*, clear) was a shrill trumpet and its call to action comes from its use as a signal in times of war. Another old version of the shawm was called a **bombard**, whose name came from a type of late medieval cannon used to hurl big stones (a name in turn taken from Latin *bombus*, booming); later the bombard became known to Germans as the **Pommer**.

Then there were the **serpent** and the **ophicleide**. The first of these got its name from the way its eight-foot length was bent into three U-shapes (its maker might be called a **serpentist**). The ophicleide was a later relative, whose name is from Greek *ophis*, serpent + *kleis*, key. This appeared in the early nineteenth century but was later replaced by the **tuba** or **euphonium** (the latter from Greek *euphōnos*, having a pleasing sound, an opinion open to dissent). The **bombardon** was a nineteenth-century kind of trumpet, rather like the ophicleide.

The most famous, and probably the most often heard, wind instrument was the **fife** (German *Pfeife*, pipe), a small, shrill flute that brings to mind the fife and drum of the old-time army marching band, so much so that **fife and drum** came to be a metaphor for the military life. Another wind instrument was called the **flageolet** or **flageolette**, of which a medieval version was called the **flagel** (from Old French *flajol*). It was rather like a modern recorder and the oddest thing about it was that the shriller types were sometimes used to teach caged birds to sing.

Incidentally, the mouthpiece of a recorder which contains the sharp lip against which the air impinges is called a **fipple**, a word which may be linked to an Icelandic word for the lip of a horse.

Of thimbleriggers
and joculators

OUTSIDE THE HOME, many other forms of entertainment were available, though participants often needed to keep their wits about them.

One especially widespread entertainment was gambling, which took place anywhere that people gathered—in markets, fairgrounds, racecourses, pubs, or in the street. Those in charge of them usually had some way of diverting the punter from his money by less than honest means.

One gambling game required a leather belt, garter or string tied into an endless loop. The man in charge twisted it into a figure-of-eight formation and asked someone to put a finger into one of the loops thus made. If the string snagged on his finger when the string was pulled away, he won. The trick was that there were two ways to make the figure-of-eight. In one, the game was genuine, with one loop snagging and the other not; in the other, neither did, and the victim always lost. In Britain, from the eighteenth century onwards, it was sometimes called **pin and girdle**, more often **prick the garter**, but it had been known from the sixteenth century and after as **fast and loose**, using *fast* in its sense of something fixed or immovable. The expression *to play fast and loose* became an idiom some time before 1557, the date of its first recorded use. It was an obvious progression from the nature of the game to a sense of dishonestly or irresponsibly trifling with another's affections.

Another gambling game was **thimblerig**, also known as **pea and thimbles** (as the **shell game** in North America, perhaps because the game was at times played with half walnut shells in place of thimbles), in which you had to guess under which of three thimbles a pea was hidden. In 1870, Andrew Steinmetz wrote of it in *The Gaming Table: Its Votaries and Victims*:

> All races, fairs, and other such conglomerations of those whom Heaven had blessed with more money than wit, used to be frequented by minor members of 'The Fancy', who are technically called flat-catchers, and who picked up a very pretty living by a quick hand, a rattling tongue, a deal board, three thimbles, and a pepper-corn. The game they played with these three curious articles is a sort of Lilliputian game at cups and balls; and the beauty of it lies in dexterously seeming to place the pepper-corn under one particular thimble, getting a green to bet that it

> was there, and then winning his money by
> showing that it is not.

Cups and balls was the larger-scale version of thimblerig. **Green** here means a naive player; a **flat-catcher** caught **flats**, Victorian slang for a mug or sucker, so named because he was the opposite of *sharp*. The sharp ones, or **sharpers**, were in charge of the games—in this case, he might be called a **thimblerigger**. He used sleight-of-hand to ensure the pea was not where it seemed to be when the punter came to make his choice. As with so many games, he often had accomplices who posed as players to work up interest, entice the flats to join in and perhaps also play a game or two to show how easy it was to win. This accomplice might be called a **bonneter** (because his job was to knock a winning punter's hat over his eyes while the operator bolted with the stakes), a **jollier** (since he jollied the punters along), **egger** (because he egged them on), or any of half a dozen other cant names. Another common name for this type of swindler or confidence trickster was **magsman**, from *mag*, a slang term for a chatterbox, good verbal skills being a vital part of the process (it may derive from **magpie**, a noisy, chattering bird).

Another gambling game was **spin-em-rounds**, usually played in the street; it was mentioned by Henry Mayhew in his *London Life and the London Poor* of 1851. Another name for it was **wheel-of-fortune**, in earlier times the name for the drum in which lottery tickets were spun before drawing. A slang dictionary of 1859 described it as

> a street game consisting of a piece of brass,
> wood, or iron, balanced on a pin and turned
> quickly around on a board, when the point, arrow
> shaped, stops at a number and decides the bet
> one way or the other.

The opportunity for cheating might seem less here, but, taking a line through crooked roulette wheels, there was no doubt much advantage to be got by a clever person in charge.

A game called **three-up** was also described by Mayhew. It was usually played in pubs:

> 'Three-up' is played fairly among the
> costermongers; but is most frequently resorted to
> when strangers are present to 'make a
> pitch',—which is, in plain words, to cheat any
> stranger who is rash enough to bet upon them...
> This adept illustrated his skill to me by throwing
> up three halfpennies, and, five times out of six,
> they fell upon the floor, whether he threw them
> nearly to the ceiling or merely to his shoulder, all
> heads or all tails. The halfpence were the proper
> current coins—indeed, they were my own; and
> the result is gained by a peculiar position of the
> coins on the fingers, and a peculiar jerk in the
> throwing.

The most famous of such crooked games is **find the lady** or the **three-card trick**, which is still widely played. Three playing cards, one of which is often the queen of hearts (hence one name for the game) or a king (known as *the gentleman*), were shown face up and then laid face down and rapidly moved about by the sharper. Somehow the mark never found the vital card. One way to disguise the final position was to collect the three cards in an open stack between the joints of thumb and second finger. With some practice, the dealer could release whichever card he wanted as he flicked your hand across the table and so confuse even someone watching closely. The game is often called **three-card monte** in North America, a name taken from **monte**, a Spanish game using 45 playing cards, which was once common in Mexico and California.

Such gambling games existed alongside street entertainers of many kinds: singers, **hurdy-gurdy** players, blind fiddlers, **joculators** (an elevated term for a jester or minstrel, from Latin *joculator*, jester), dancing dogs, **engastrimyths** (another posh term, for a ventriloquist, from Greek *en*, in + *gaster*, belly + *muthos*, speech), and performers of strange and exotic feats of strength and endurance.

Street entertainment in London at the end of the nineteenth century was recalled by Thomas Burke in his *London in my Time*:

> At one point you would find a Highlander
> (probably from Camden Town) with bagpipes, and

> a lady partner doing the sword dance. A few yards
> away a man and woman doing a thought-reading
> act. Then a trained horse spelling 'corn' and 'hay'
> from lettered cards. ... Then a **one-man band**—a
> man who carried and worked with mouth and with
> different limbs, a big drum, a triangle, Pan-pipes,
> cymbals, and concertina. Then a **contortionist**
> and **escapist** being roped and manacled. Then a
> weight-lifter; an Italian woman with a cage of
> fortune-telling budgerigars; a tattooed sailor
> advertising a **tattooist**—in short, a small
> Bartholomew Fair every Saturday night, and a
> gusto to it which is, or seems to be, absent even
> from the Bank Holiday Fairs of to-day.

He might also have mentioned the **hokey-pokey man**, who sold ice cream on the street, with his cry of "Hokey-pokey, a penny a lump!", whose name may be from *hocus-pocus*, though some have pointed instead to the Italian *O che poco!* meaning "Oh, how little!" Incidentally, the dance called the *hokey-cokey* ("You do the hokey-cokey and you turn around. That's what it's all about") was originally the *hokey-pokey* or perhaps the *hokee-pokee*, definitely from *hocus-pocus*. Other foods were sold by the **muffin-man**, who in the winter usually sold crumpets instead, and the **orange-girls** of street and theatre, of whom Nell Gwyn is the most famous.

James Greenwood records asking a workhouse master in his *Mysteries of Modern London* of 1883 about performers fallen on bad times coming through his doors. He remarked:

> We have at present in the house two families of
> acrobats, a sword-swallower, the fellow that eats
> burning tow with a fork, [and] the black man who
> throws the half-hundred weight.

But he went on to say,

> I am quite sure that all the years I have filled the
> office of master I never once entered a **Punch-
> and-Judy man** on the parish books... Which I
> take to be a very remarkable circumstance when
> one bears in mind that any time during the last
> quarter of a century Punch has been supposed to
> be on his last legs.

What had vanished, he commented, was the **gallanty show** (possibly from the Italian *galante*, courteous or honourable, that also gave us *gallant*), which Punch and Judy men of a previous generation had found to be a good way of earning money after dark. It was a shadow-puppet show, using silhouette figures projected on a white sheet stretched across the front of the booth, with a lantern or candles behind.

Another common public entertainment in towns and cities was the theatre or music hall. In the eighteenth and early nineteenth century, any sort of cheap public entertainment of this sort was a **gaff** (from Romany *gav*, town), a word that could equally be applied to a fair or exhibition. The cheapest sort of entertainment, a low-life relative of the music hall, was the **penny-gaff**, from the price of admission. Every investigator who entered and described such places was appalled. This is Richard Rowe, writing in his *Life in the London Streets* of 1881:

> Two floors of a house had been knocked into one
> to form the concert-room. Rough wooden seats,
> rising at the end of the room nearest the door,
> with a villanously dark, dirty, narrow, and
> malodorous passage behind the same, were
> devoted to those disposed to pay only a penny for
> their entertainment.

A cheap theatre that presented lurid melodrama was given the slang name of a **blood-tub**, from the vessel into which a slaughtered animal's blood was drained. It turns up in *Hilda Lessways*, by Arnold Bennett, dated 1911:

> "I'd no idea there was a theatre in Bursley," she
> remarked idly, driven into a banality by the press
> of her sensations. "They used to call it the Blood
> Tub," he replied. "Melodrama and murder and
> gore—you know."

The English once had public entertainments that we regard today with fascinated horror. In 1859, some were recalled in his book *Gaslight and Daylight* by George Sala:

> Every Englishman who numbers more than forty
> summers, can remember what formed the staple
> objects of amusement among the people in his
> youth. Bull-baiting, bear-baiting, duck-hunting,
> floating a cat in a bowl pursued by dogs;

> fastening two cats together by their tails, and
> then swinging them across a horizontal pole to
> see which should first kill the other; tying a
> cat and an owl together and throwing them
> into the water to fight it out; cock-fighting
> (before lords in drawing-rooms, sometimes—the
> birds being provided with silver spurs); ratting;
> and, as a climax of filthy savagery, worrying
> matches by men against bull-dogs, the man
> being on his knees having his hands tied behind
> him!

Bear-baiting is recorded in an illustration in the *Luttrell Psalter* of about 1325, in which a chained bear is being set upon by four dogs. By Shakespeare's time, Londoners usually went south of the river to the unregulated suburb of Southwark for such entertainments. The notorious Paris Gardens on Bankside were near the Globe Theatre and contained two sites, also called theatres, one for bear-baiting, the other for **bull-baiting**. It seems the clientele to all three was similar. Though the end was hardly in doubt for the bears and bulls, it was by no means an unequal contest, since they were trained up to give a good account of themselves. However, it was often necessary to provoke bulls by blowing pepper up their noses. We still have *bulldogs*, originally bred and trained to bait bulls.

A related sport was **cockfighting**, usually carried out in small, noisy enclosed spaces called **cockpits**, a term that survives in everyday speech for not entirely unrelated spaces on ships and aircraft and in racing cars, and in the *pit* of the theatres that once served double duty as animal-baiting enclosures. Here the sport was less unequal still, since the **fighting cocks** were closely matched to ensure an even contest (**fighting cock** became a slang term for a man with courage and spirit; another slang term from the pastime was **cock of the walk**). The surface of the pit was often grass, and was commonly known as **the sod**, a term that was transferred to the sport itself, as we still say **the turf** for horse racing. It generated a whole vocabulary of terms that have now vanished: a **gablock** or **gavelock** was a metal spur (from Old English *gafeluc*, fork), another name for it was **gaff**, a different word entirely to the earlier one, this time from Provençal *gaf*, hook, which is also the source of our *gaffe* for an unfortunate error); a **heeler** was a fighting cock, that used his spurs or *heels*; a cock that **shot the pit** rushed out of the cockpit from cowardice; a **shake-bag** was a cock turned out of a bag to fight an opponent unseen or unmatched (which led to *shake-bag* being a term of the late eighteenth century for somebody of low reputation); a **stive** or **stove** was a straw enclosure to keep the cock warm between bouts; and so on. The **cock-penny** was once well known in the north of England; a directory of Westmoreland in 1851 noted that:

> The schoolmaster also receives the rents of the market house, and of the old school, and likewise a cock penny given by each scholar on Shrove Tuesday.

This was said to be a substitute for bringing a cock to school on that day for a fight.

Classical scholars of the seventeenth century created elevated terms for some of these activities, based on Greek *makhē*, battle. So cockfighting was **alectryomachy**, from Greek *alektroin*, cockerel, and **cynarctomachy** was bear-baiting using dogs (Greek *kuōn*, dog + *arktos*, bear). However, **tauromachy** (Greek *tauros*, bull) was bullfighting, not bull-baiting, for which a scholarly term doesn't seem to have been invented.

These and other sports of similar kind, such as **badger-baiting** and **dogfighting**, which had mostly become the entertainments of the working man, were officially outlawed in Britain by an Act of Parliament of 1835 under agitation from the body then called the Society for the Prevention of Cruelty to Animals, though cockfighting and dogfighting both continue to a limited extent clandestinely. Legislation to outlaw *hare coursing*, *stag-hunting*, and *fox-hunting* with dogs only came into effect in 2005; time will tell whether these terms strike many of us in the same way that bear-baiting does now.

Natural magic

WE LIVE in an age of technological entertainment —films, television, radio, CDs. Their roots go back further than you might guess.

"Kellogg & Co.'s Great War show is coming," proclaimed an advert in a Michigan newspaper in March 1867, shortly after the end of the Civil War (or "the late unpleasantness", as people euphemized it). "This is no Magic Lantern or Peep Show, but a Genuine Drummond Light Stereopticon, capable of producing the Programme on more than 100,000 square feet of brilliantly illuminated canvass, and the only Panorama in America where thousands of soldiers have recognized the fields on which they have fought."

We would be disappointed, were we to be transported back in time to see this spectacle, to discover that it was just a slide show, although, to judge from the term *Drummond Light*, it was one in which the projectors were powered by the oxyhydrogen **limelight** that Captain Drummond of the Royal Engineers had invented nearly half a century earlier. A **stereopticon** was a pair of **magic lanterns**, as slide projectors were called then, mounted and operated together to create dissolves between one image and another. Its name is from Greek *stereo*, solid or three-dimensional (which we also have in *stereophonic* and similar words) + *optikon*, relating to vision.

To give a Greek name to such a device was part of the game. The creators of such early imaging techniques put as much effort into creating names for their devices as they did into inventing them. Virtually all of them turned to the classical languages for their inspiration. That was partly because the classics still had a hold on educated men, partly as a way of providing a learned gloss to their endeavours, and partly an easy way to give a veneer of bombastic self-congratulation and promotional pizzazz to their creations.

The **peep show** mentioned in the advertisement now has implications of a near-pornographic display that were absent at the time. When they first appeared, in the eighteenth century, showmen called them by the grander name **prospective views** or **vues d'optiques**. They were coloured images lit from behind and placed in a box with a small hole in the front, which people paid a small sum to look into. Though these became common by the end of the eighteenth century, the name *peep show* wasn't attached to them until the middle of the next. They were common in the street and in fairgrounds. In *Mysteries of*

Modern London, by James Greenwood, 1883, he describes what he calls a **peepshowman**:

> Quite as familiar as the little theatre with its four slender wooden legs and its green-baise petticoat was the individual who carried his panoramic box on his back, and the trestles to stand it on in his hand, and who was sure of an audience, albeit not always a paying one, within two minutes of his making a 'pitch'. It was a marvellously cheap entertainment at a halfpenny, and it had the advantage of combining instruction with amusement.

The mental association with **What the Butler Saw** machines and others like them later caused the term to acquire its salacious undertones, which it certainly had by the time that H G Wells published *Love and Mr Lewisham* in 1900:

> Try as we may to stay those delightful moments, they fade and pass remorselessly; there is no returning, no recovering, only—for the foolish—the vilest peep-shows and imitations in dens and darkened rooms.

In its earliest appearances, in the seventeenth century, the second part of *magic lantern* was written **lanthorn**. The oldest spellings came from French *lanterne* (ultimately from Greek *lampter*, torch or lamp). English speakers thought this must be wrong and changed the last part to *horn*, since most lanterns of the time had windows made from very thin sheets of cow's horn. The early magic lanterns, such as those of Athanasius Kircher in the late 1600s, could evoke an emotion akin to dread. As Edward Phillips put it in the 1696 edition of his *New World of English Words*:

> A Magic Lanthorn, a certain small Optical
> Macheen, that shews by a gloomy Light upon a
> white Wall, Spectres and Monsters so hideous,
> that he who knows not the Secret, believes it to
> be perform'd by Magick Art.

Even the rational late eighteenth century wasn't immune to such emotions, a fact traded on by various hustlers who made enhancements to the device. A Monsieur de Philippsthal (as his name was given in an advertisement in the *Times* in December 1801, though he was actually a German named Paul Philipsthal) opened an exhibition at the Lyceum in the Strand in London called a "Grand Cabinet of Optical and Mechanical Illusions". By moving the projector backwards and forwards on rails, figures were made to increase and decrease in size, advance and retreat, dissolve, vanish, and pass into each other. Philipsthal called his show the **Phantasmagoria**, borrowed from the French *fantasmagorie*, which itself came from *fantasme*, phantasm, plus the Greek *agora*, a place of assembly. However, as the *Oxford English Dictionary* says, a little sniffily, he may have merely wanted "a mouth-filling and startling term" and strict etymology be damned.

The British physicist Sir David Brewster (who, incidentally, invented the **kaleidoscope** in 1817, naming it from Greek *kalos*, beautiful + *eidos*, form + *skopein*, to look at) described Philipsthal's exhibition in his *Natural Magic* in 1831:

> Spectres, skeletons, and terrific figures ...
> suddenly advanced upon the spectators,
> becoming larger as they approached them, and
> finally vanished by appearing to sink into the
> ground.

By all accounts the images were devilishly convincing. In fact Philipsthal was building on 20 years of experience of such techniques in Belgium and France and soon many other showmen competed with him, linguistically as well as entrepreneurially: Mark Lonsdale presented a **Spectrographia** at the Lyceum in 1802; a Mr Meeson offered a phantasmagoria at Bartholomew Fair in 1803; and a series of optical **Eidothaumata** (Greek *eidos*, form or resemblance + *thauma*, a wonder or marvel) were to be seen at the Lyceum in 1804.

The Irishman Robert Barker, a painter of portraits and miniatures, invented an image large enough to encircle the viewer, the first one being a view of London that he exhibited in premises off Leicester Square in 1792. This is where another word from our American advertisement comes in: the **panorama**, which was Mr Barker's second attempt at naming it (his first go was **La Nature à Coup d'Oeil**, nature at a glance, but he soon realized it was an uncommercial title). *Panorama* is from Greek *pan*, all, and *horama*, a view. Panoramas became very popular in the nine-teenth century, particularly so in the US, sometimes being as much as 300 feet long and 50 feet high. This explains the joke I found in a Connecticut newspaper of 1899:

> If you don't believe that art is long, visit a
> panorama.

They included some that advanced on rollers to give an illusion of movement. The American ones were often called **cycloramas** (Greek *kuklos*, circle) a term first recorded in the 1840s but which is now usually reserved for the illuminated curved backcloth of a theatre stage; a later version was the **diorama** (Greek *dia*, through), invented by Louis Daguerre and Charles Bouton, which from 1823 operated in a specially built theatre in Regent's Park, London; this had a revolving floor (to accommodate the audience, not the display) and was described by the *Times*'s re-viewer as an immeasurable improvement on the panorama. These days, *panorama* has inverted its meaning to refer instead to the landscapes that Robert Barker so successfully simulated; *diorama* is now a general term for three-dimensional set pieces, usually in museums.

One of the early viewing devices for perspective prints, contain-ing a lens and mirror on a stand, was named the **Zograscope** for reasons now lost to us (possibly from Greek *zographos*, painter, or conceivably from *zogrion*, menagerie), though it was also called more prosaically a **diagonal mirror** or an **optical pillar machine**. The image was placed on a table and viewed through a large lens, whose curving edges supplied a surprisingly good sensation of depth. Surviving examples were often designed for the drawing rooms of well-off eighteenth-century families desiring the very latest in imaging technology for their after-dinner soirées, and who wanted, in the words of a catalogue of 1784, to view at a shilling uncoloured or two shillings coloured,

> remarkable Views of Shipping, eminent Cities, Towns, Royal Palaces, Noblemen and Gentleman's Seats and Gardens in Great Britain, France and Holland, Views of Venice, Florence, Ancient and Modern Rome, and the most striking public Buildings in and about London.

Around this time, parlour pastimes included the **myriorama**, which consisted of a series of small pictures that could be assembled in many different ways to create scenic views, hence the name—from *myriad*, derived from Greek *murias*, a very large number; an American encyclopedia of the period correctly stated that with 16 cards 20,922,789,888,000 combinations were possible, surely a large enough number to justify the name. From the 1830s, the *myriorama* was also a public entertainment in Britain, toured by a Mr C W Poole, which in 1897 is recorded as celebrating its diamond jubilee by visiting Liverpool, Plymouth, and Bristol.

Though these images were moved about in cunning ways, they remained static pictures, not animated as we would expect today. Many attempts were made to create a proper moving image, all of them depending on a phenomenon called persistence of vision, which relies on the eye's ability to retain an image for a brief moment after the object has vanished. Around 1825 the **thaumatrope** was invented (once again from Greek *thauma*, marvel + *-tropos*, turning), which consisted of a disc with two related but different pictures on the two sides; when rotated quickly the two images merged into one—you can still find examples as children's toys today, the classic one having a canary and a cage on the two sides so that by spinning the disc you can seem to put the bird in its cage. In 1832, the Belgian physicist Joseph Plateau introduced a development, variously called a **phenakistoscope** (Greek *phenakiotis*, a cheat or imposter), **fantoscope**, or **phantasmascope**; this consisted of a rotating wheel, with slots cut in it and a series of drawings on the back; when rotated and viewed with a mirror through the slots, a moving image was created. Two years later, William Horner invented what he called the **Daedulum**, the wheel of the Devil; it became much better known later in the century under the name of **zoetrope** (a name formed irregularly from Greek *zoē*, life + *-tropos*, turning) or **wheel of life**. It was a slotted cylinder with a series of pictures on the inner surface; when viewed through the slits with the cylinder rotating, it gave an impression of continuous motion.

In 1877 Emile Reynaud in Paris created what was later described as "an ingenious adaptation of the zoetrope", which he called the **praxinoscope** (another badly formed word, from the Greek *praxis*, action). This used a series of mirrors in the centre of the drum instead of the slots to provide a better-quality and brighter image without the distortion of the zoetrope; with this system it was possible to project the images on a screen, a step nearer practical cinematography. A further modification of this device, the **zoöpraxiscope** (Green *zoion*, animal), was used by Eadweard Muybridge to project his pioneering moving pictures of a horse, which resolved the ancient dispute whether a galloping horse ever has all four feet off the ground at once (it does).

It was Muybridge who got Thomas Alva Edison interested in moving pictures, through trying to persuade him to find a way of linking the zoöpraxiscope with Edison's new phonograph. Edison went a different way, creating his **kinetoscope** (Greek *kinetos*, movable), which used a series of images on celluloid film (created using a **kinetograph**, an early film camera) which ran on rollers inside a cabinet; one person at a time viewed the result through a lens at the top. A reporter visited Edison's famous workshop in April 1894 and was shown the device by Edison's assistant William Dickson, who had developed the device:

> An electric light was burning inside and the noise
> of rapidly running machinery was audible. The
> scene that was reproduced was that of a barber

> shop, and a placard on the wall informed the
> observer that it was 'The Latest Wonder, Shave
> and Hair Cut for a Nickel.' It pictured a man being
> shaved while two others sat by and enjoyed a joke
> which one of them had discovered in a comic
> paper.

Not perhaps the stuff of Academy Awards, but a marvel of the times.

In 1894, Herman Casler patented the **mutograph** (assumed to be from Latin *mutare*, to change) a device for taking a series of pictures of an object in motion, which were then viewed with a **mutoscope**. Turning a handle caused a series of individual images to flip past, giving a semblance of motion (those *What the Butler Saw* machines I mentioned earlier, once a staple of British seaside piers, were a type of mutoscope). But technically this was a dead end and the future lay with ideas like those of Edison.

PART 4

Transport
& Fashion

Your carriage awaits

WE'VE ALMOST FORGOTTEN the era of horse-drawn transport, though it ended less than a century ago. These days, we're most likely to be reminded of it through reading the fiction of earlier times, such as that of Sir Arthur Conan Doyle.

So many investigations began with a carriage pulling up outside 221b Baker Street:

> As he spoke there was the sharp sound of horses' hoofs and grating wheels against the curb, followed by a sharp pull at the bell. Holmes whistled. "A pair, by the sound," said he. "Yes," he continued, glancing out of the window. "A nice little brougham and a pair of beauties. A hundred and fifty guineas apiece. There's money in this case, Watson, if there is nothing else."

So began in earnest *A Scandal in Bohemia* in the *Strand Magazine* in July 1891.

It had to be a man of means driving that **brougham**—it was definitely a private conveyance for the socially advantaged, not only for "dukes and marquises, and people of that sort", as *Household Words* (in the person of Charles Dickens) noted in 1851, but also for members of the prosperous middle classes; if you called in a society doctor for a home consultation, it was a fair bet he would arrive in a brougham. It was a one- or two-horse closed four-wheeled carriage, compact and manoeuvrable, the horse-era equivalent of a town car. Its name commemorates a former Lord Chancellor, the Scotsman Henry Brougham, later the first Baron Brougham and Vaux, a brilliant and genial man, famous in his time but forgotten now.

Later in the same story, Irene Adler arrives at Briony Lodge in a **landau**. This could be pulled by four horses (a **four-in-hand**, from the four sets of reins held by the driver), though two was more common. It was a low-slung vehicle with four seats facing each other in pairs, usually open but with folding tops front and rear that could be raised and closed together in bad weather. The landau was an excellent vehicle for being seen in, which is why it features in so many pictures of royalty or lord mayors in ceremonial processions even today. It's named after Landau in Germany, where it was invented in the eighteenth century.

A related vehicle makes a fleeting appearance in *The Adventure of Shoscombe Old Place*:

> Within a quarter of an hour we saw the big open
> yellow barouche coming down the long avenue,
> with two splendid, high-stepping gray carriage
> horses in the shafts.

The **barouche** was just as posh as the landau but it had just
the one folding top, at the rear, with the two backward-facing
seats behind the driver open to the elements. The name comes
from the German dialect word *Barutsche* which derives via Italian
from Latin *birotus*, two-wheeled. Along the etymological route
from Latin two extra wheels were added, which reminds us not
to rely on a word's history for its meaning. It was definitely a
vehicle to aspire to, as Jane Austen made plain in *Sense and Sens-
ibility* in 1811:

> His mother wished to interest him in political
> concerns, to get him into parliament, or to see
> him connected with some of the great men of the
> day. Mrs John Dashwood wished it likewise; but
> in the mean while, till one of these superior
> blessings could be attained, it would have
> quieted her ambition to see him driving a
> barouche.

Whenever Holmes and Watson needed to rush off to some
exotic location, such as Norwood or Leatherhead, their first
action was frequently the same as modern men in a hurry—they
called a **cab**. These were horse-driven, of course: motorized ones
didn't appear in any numbers in London until 1905. *Cab* was a
contraction of **cabriolet**, a light two-wheeled vehicle drawn by

one horse. These had been around since the middle of the seventeenth century in France, but had first appeared for hire in London in 1823 (and were being called *cabs* by 1827 at the latest). The name shares an origin with the ballet leap *cabriole*; both derive from French *cabrioler*, to leap in the air like a goat, which was taken from Latin *caper*, goat, which is also the origin of our verb meaning to leap about in a lively or playful way. The French called the carriage a *cabriole* because of its curious bouncy motion. Conan Doyle never uses the full term in the Sherlock Holmes stories, since by the time he was writing, near the end of the nineteenth century, *cabriolet* was rare (though its name was revived later for a couple of types of motor car). Its abbreviation had been generalized to refer to a number of vehicles, both two- and four-wheeled, that had in common that they were available for hire on the street.

The classic one, which is familiar to anyone who has ever seen a period film or television programme, was the **hansom**. This had been invented by the man who designed Birmingham Town Hall, Joseph Hansom. He patented his safety cab on 23 December 1834, with the intention of making an existing two-wheeled vehicle safer by preventing it tipping over after an accident. His vehicles were built on a square framework on two wheels each 7½ feet in diameter. The hansom cabs in the Sherlock Holmes stories didn't actually incorporate many of Hansom's ideas but they kept his name (it was almost Hansom's only legacy, since he never made much money out of his invention and building the town hall bankrupted him). The **cabman** sat high up at the back—in the open air, as all drivers did at the period—and talked to his passengers through a small hatch in the roof.

A four-wheeled cab based on the brougham was named the **clarence**, after the then Duke of Clarence, later William IV, but acquired the slang name of **growler**, from the noise its steel-rimmed wheels made on the road. Holmes, as befits a man who could identify 140 varieties of tobacco ash, was familiar with the type and applied his deductive skills in *A Study in Scarlet*:

> I satisfied myself that it was a cab and not a private carriage by the narrow gauge of the wheels. The ordinary London growler is considerably less wide than a gentleman's brougham.

A slightly larger version had four wheels and so was boringly known as a **four-wheeler**; it features in *A Case of Identity*, in which the wonderfully named Mr Hosmer Angel disappears:

> Hosmer came for us in a hansom, but as there were two of us he put us both into it and stepped himself into a four-wheeler, which happened to be the only other cab in the street.

Another word that never occurs in the Sherlock Holmes stories is **taxi**, because it didn't appear in the language until 1907. It's an abbreviation of *taximeter* (from French *taxe*, tariff), a device for measuring the fee to be paid that had started to appear in cabs in London in 1898 (to start with it was called a *taxameter*, from German *Taxe*, a tax; the cabs had previously been popular in both Paris and Berlin). Motorized cabs had them from the start and what to call them was a problem. In 1907, the *Daily Chronicle* remarked that "Every journalist ... has his idea of what the vehicle should be called" and went on to list *taxi*, *motor-cab*, *taxi-cab*, and *taximo* among the options touted. But by February 1908, the same newspaper was able to report that "Within the past few months the 'taxi' has been the name given to the motor-cab." In full, *taxi* was *taximeter cabriolet*, a term well worth abbreviating.

An official name for the taxi, today as then, is **hackney carriage** (in many cities their licensing is controlled by the relevant *hackney carriage office*). **Hackney** is from the London inner-city area, but by a convoluted route. In medieval times it was a little village way out of town. It had a reputation for the riding horses bred there—*ambling horses* as they were then known, to distinguish them from war horses. It came to refer to hired horses at about the end of the fourteenth century, because such horses were often available for hire. Later still, the emphasis shifted from "horse" to "hire", and *hackney* also came to be used for any passenger vehicle that was similarly available. Both horse and carriage also became in brief a **hack**. Hackney horses were commonplace; as a result something that appeared so frequently as

to have lost freshness and interest was described from the eighteenth century on as *hackneyed*. And since such horses were often
worked extremely hard and hired out to anybody who wanted
them, *hack* came also to refer to a person who could be commissioned for any kind of drudge work, especially in reference to
Grub Street scribblers prepared to write anything at all that
would scrape a meagre living (modern journalists wear the
badge with pride).

Holmes and Watson are never recorded as riding in the conveyance of the proletariat, the humble London **bus**, though
some other characters do. Nor does Conan Doyle use the fuller
term **omnibus**, a word that for us today is known only from the
registered names of a few firms that run buses, such as the
Southern Vectis Omnibus Company on the Isle of Wight. It
started out in French in 1828 as part of the name for a new type of
public transport that was open to everyone, of any social class. It
was a long coach with seats down each side, called a *voiture
omnibus*, a carriage for everyone, where *omnibus* is the dative plural
of the Latin *omnis*, all. (The Shakespearean stage direction, *exeunt
omnes*, everybody leaves, includes another form of the same
word.) The idea, and the word, were soon brought over into
England and English. *Saunders' Newsletter* of 4 July 1829 noted:

> The new vehicle, called the omnibus, commenced
> running this morning from Paddington to the
> City.

You will note the French phrase had already been shortened (*voiture* was obviously foreign rubbish, but *omnibus* was classical and we could live with that). By 1832, it had been shortened further to today's *bus*, a weird linguistic invention that consists just of part of the Latin ending *-ibus*, with no root word in it at all.

Types and makes of horse-drawn carriages were then as varied as makes of car are today. Among others that Conan Doyle has his heroes travel in are the **gig**

> ("I had descended from my gig and was standing in front of him, when I saw his eyes fix themselves over my shoulder, and stare past me with an expression of the most dreadful horror"—*The Hound of the Baskervilles*).

This was a light two-wheeled one-horse open carriage, in word-history terms a flighty girl, since that was a much older sense, itself borrowed from a more literal sense of something that whirled, such as one of those old children's tops that were spun by being whipped with a string. Another two-wheeler was the **dog-cart**, with open seats placed back to back across the body of the vehicle, given that name because at one time it incorporated a box under the seat for sportsmen's dogs. The **wagonette**

> ("The train pulled up at a small wayside station and we all descended. Outside, beyond the low, white fence, a wagonette with a pair of cobs was

waiting"—again from *The Hound of the Baskervilles*)

was a larger four-wheeled cart with a seat or bench at each side facing inwards. (A *cob* was a short-legged, stout variety of horse, probably from the old word meaning stout, rounded, or sturdy that's also the source of *cobnut*, another name for a hazelnut.) The **trap** was a variant of the gig, whose distinguishing feature was that it was on springs to ease the ride, not always successfully to judge from the creation in the 1830s of **rattle-trap** for a vehicle that gave a rough ride.

The methods of transport that Conan Doyle doesn't mention likewise make up a substantial list, since he and his readers are more interested in the developing story than in an obsessive interest in how his characters get from place to place. He might have mentioned the **victoria**, a low four-wheeled pleasure carriage for two with a folding top and a raised seat in front for the driver (named after Her Gracious Majesty); the **governess-cart**, a light two-wheeled vehicle with seats face to face at the sides (not by any means always used by governesses); the **sociable** (short for **sociable-coach**), a larger vehicle for pleasure trips; the **phaeton** (from the Greek *Phaethon*, sun of Helios the sun-god, who got into such trouble driving his father's sun-chariot), a light, open, four-wheeled horse-drawn carriage; the **tilbury** (from the name of the inventor, not the place in Essex), a similar carriage fashionable rather earlier in the century;

and finally the **charabanc** (from French *char-à-bancs*, literally "carriage with benches"), a long open vehicle with transverse seats looking forward, which had been known since the early nineteenth century, but which in its motor-coach incarnation in the early twentieth century carried trippers on excursions. H G Wells made plain his disdain for the type in his story *The New Accelerator* of 1903:

> He gripped my arm and, walking at such a pace that he forced me into a trot, went shouting with me up the hill. A whole char-à-banc-ful of people turned and stared at us in unison after the manner of people in chars-à-banc.

Ruffs, and cuffs, and farthingales and things

FASHION GENERATES and discards more vocabulary than almost any other area of life. A good way to illustrate both changing fashion and the changing language of fashion is to go back to the time of Shakespeare.

The Elizabethan period was more effervescent and exaggerated in fashion than any other in history. Pictures show us extraordinarily foppish attitudes in fashions, male and female alike, against which William Harrison railed in his *Description of England* in 1587—in the curmudgeonly way of elderly men of every generation who think the country's going to the dogs, but in this case with some justification—complaining of the "costliness", "the excess and the vanity", and "the fickleness and the folly" of the costume of his time.

For women, the main fashion items of the period were the "ruffs, and cuffs, and farthingales" which in *The Taming of the Shrew* Petruchio teasingly promises Katherine she might be allowed to wear. The least remarkable of these, you may feel, are the **cuffs**, hardly worth his mentioning them. But the cuffs of upper-class women's clothes were then often highly ornate items that could be bought and worn separately.

The **farthingale** had been introduced from Spain around 1545. The name has nothing to do with the obsolete coin called a farthing; it's from Spanish *verdugo*, meaning a rod or stick, via *verdugado* for the garment, a term which the English transformed into something more memorable and sensible-sounding at the small price of etymological confusion. The sticks were actually hoops of wicker or whalebone, sometimes wire, made progressively larger towards the bottom, sewn into a canvas support to create a conical or bell shape as a support for the skirts on top. From the 1570s, a padded roll of cloth under the skirt was added that threw it out at the sides and back; this had the unprepossessing name of **bum roll**. *Bum* was indeed known then—in fact, from at least two centuries earlier still, though where it came from isn't known—but it wasn't as mildly rude as it became later; it turns up in a bit of comedy by Puck in *A Midsummer Night's Dream*:

> The wisest aunt, telling the saddest tale,
> Sometime for three-foot stool mistaketh me;
> Then slip I from her bum, down topples she.

Yet another extraordinary version, imported from the continent in the 1590s, was what historians of costume call the **wheel farthingale** (in a play called *North-ward Hoe* in 1607, Thomas Dekker referred to it as a **Catherine-wheel farthingale**—light blue touch paper and retire) which stood out like a platform around the hips, with the skirt falling from it in the shape of an outsized hat box. Its awfulness as an item of clothing was to some extent mitigated by ladies' being able to rest their arms on it. The fashion survived Elizabeth I, though Queen Anne, wife of her successor King James VI of Scotland (James I to the English), was said to have worn one four feet wide at the hips.

The other item Petruchio mentions, the **ruff**, was a unisex item. Men wore these heavily frilled collars in even larger sizes than the women and they grew larger as the sixteenth century proceeded. "They not only continue their great ruffs still," complained Philip Stubbes in his *Anatomie of Abuses* of 1573, "but also use them bigger than ever they did." They started life in a small way as another imported Spanish fashion, for ruffles, and it seems that *ruff* is a contracted form of *ruffle*. The latter is from an older verb meaning to spoil the neat arrangement of something (today we might on occasion still ruffle some feathers, more often figuratively than literally) and later to form small bends or folds, as in those of the ruff. One of its linguistic relatives was the old German *rüffelen*, to crumple or **goffer**. Though the Elizabethan servant would have goffered her master's or mistress's ruffs—with many yards of material in each one, it could be quite a job—she wouldn't have known this word, since it only came into English a century later (from French *gaufrer*, to stamp with a patterned tool, which is a close relative through German of *waffle* and *wafer*). A **goffering iron** is a heated implement for putting the curls and crimps into lace and frills. Victorian laundrymaids knew goffering irons all too well and they're still around, though hardly an everyday household item, thank heavens.

From about 1580, the ruff was converted into a stiffly wired, wide collar that could stand high behind the head. This was a **rebato** or **rabato** (from medieval French *rabat*, literally the act of turning something down), another accessory that was worn by both men and women. These collars often had a deeply scalloped edge in an intricate pattern, from the early 1600s called a **piccadil** (or, if you prefer, **pickadil** or **picadill**—the spelling was, and still is, variable). This name is intimately linked with the geography of London. A tailor named Robert Baker had a shop in the Strand at the time and acquired a fortune from making and selling piccadils. Around 1612 he built a fine house on open country to the west of London. This was nicknamed Piccadilly Hall, either from the source of the tailor's wealth, or because it was at the edge of his property, as the piccadils were at the edge of items of clothing. The nickname stuck and gave its name to the street called Piccadilly and to Piccadilly Circus.

An alternative to the ruff was **falling-bands**. A *band* was specifically the collar of a shirt or similar garment (ruffs were held in place by cords called **band-strings**). Falling-bands were wide collars of linen or lace that lay across each shoulder and in later times down on to the chest. Yet again, both men and women wore them, though in different styles. Much later, the bands became simplified again into a pair of strips that hung down in front, the **bands** of a lawyer's or clergyman's formal dress.

So much costume was shared between the sexes in this period that it provoked William Harrison to another burst of indignation:

> I have met with some of these trulls in London so
> disguised that it hath passed my skill to discern
> whether they were men or women.

(A **trull** was a prostitute, from German *Trulle*.) He also mentions women wearing **galligaskins**,

> to bear out their bums and make their attire to fit
> plum-round (as they term it).

I assume that these were actually the bum-rolls mentioned earlier, since women didn't usually wear galligaskins. They were a kind of breeches, spreading out from a slim waist to end about mid-thigh. The word was from the French *gargesque*, taken in turn from Italian *grechesca*, something Greek, because the fashion for loose breeches was originally from that country. At one time, it was wrongly thought that the word came from *Gallic Gascons*, the inhabitants of Gascony, but that's a classic word-history folk tale.

Englishmen knew galligaskins were often worn by sailors, so they assumed that the first part was *galley*, either from the oared ship or from the cooking area on board ship. Similar clothing was known at about the same time as **gally-breeches** or **gally-slops** (*slop* is a word of obscure origin that originally meant any sort of loose outer garment). *Gally-slops* was often abbreviated to **slops**, which came to refer specifically to a type of loose breeches reaching just below the knee. Much later, the shipboard garments given these names were not breeches but the more practical half-masted loose trousers; the material to make them was stored in the *slop-chest*.

Earlier in Elizabeth's reign, men wore **trunk-hose**, extremely short garments that reached no lower than the upper thigh, but which were excessively padded out to make a ring from waist to hip that matched the copiousness of women's farthingales, so much so that historians of costume call them **pumpkin hose**. They were often **paned**, formed of stripes of various colour cloth. The padding might be wool, horsehair, short linen fibres called tow, sometimes even bran, which was embarrassing if the trunk-hose sprang a leak. Another common padding was **bombast** (French *bombace*, traceable back to Latin *bombyx*, silkworm), which despite its Latin origin was actually cotton. The padding of male garments reached such a pitch in the later sixteenth century that *bombast* took on the sarcastic sense of verbal padding, high-sounding language with little meaning, that it retains in **bombastic**. (The Latin word is also the source of **bombazine**, a fabric that in Victorian times was often dyed black and used for mourning clothes: think of Queen Victoria after the death of Prince Albert.)

Below the trunk-hose, a man might wear **canions** (from Spanish *cañon* for a tube, pipe, or gun-barrel), close-fitting breeches which extended down to the knee. Below that were the **netherstocks**, long knitted or woven stockings of wool, linen, or silk. The whole assemblage, breeches and stockings together, was called **hose**, with the upper part being the **upper stock**. The oldest sense of *stock* was a tree trunk, post, or block of wood, which is why the method of punishment called the *stocks* got its name; quite how it came to be used for part of the hose is mysterious, unless people thought of the legs as tree trunks, but we do know that it's also the source of **stocking**. Around 1580-1620 another type of highly fashionable breeches were called **chausses en tonnelet** or **Venetians**, the latter because the fashion for them had been imported from Venice. These were less flounced than others and tapered slimly from the waist to just below the knee.

Above the hose, the usual male garment was the **doublet**, a padded jacket that was close-fitting and short, from the Old French word for something folded, so doubled over, which could also refer to a fur-lined coat. Some two centuries later **singlet** was created from it by analogy to refer to a simpler one-piece undergarment. The combination was often called **doublet and hose**, especially when it was worn without a cloak for some active pursuit. The two were fastened together by lots of cords called **points**. By the 1580s, the doublet had developed a low pointed waist that was compared to the shape of a pea pod and was called a **peasecod belly**. (*Pease* was the first form of pea, as in *pease pudding*, mentioned earlier. A *cod* was then a container or bag and was used rudely for the scrotum, so that the *cods* were the testicles and the **codpiece** was a bagged appendage to trunk-hose and other sorts of breeches that covered their front opening.)

Cloth of ages

FASHION CONSTANTLY CRIES OUT for innovation in fabrics as much as in style, colour, or cut. A vast range of materials has been used at various periods in the natural fabrics of silk, cotton, and wool.

Many names for fabrics commemorate the place where they were originally made, though the ability of the English to contort foreign place names has rendered them in most cases unrecognizable. Modern wearers of **jeans**, to take a classic case, are wearing garments first made from a twilled cotton fabric imported from the Italian city of *Genoa*; today, they're made from **denim**, originally the French *serge de Nîmes*, a cloth from *Nîmes*, a city in southern France. Another cotton fabric, **calico**, perpetuates a modified form of the name of the Indian port *Calicut*, from which the Portuguese exported it in the sixteenth century; yet another, **muslin**, takes its name via French and Italian from *Mussolo* (modern *Mosul*) in Iraq; **cambric** is named after a Flemish form of *Cambrai* in northern France. **Lawn** is from *Laon* in France, at one time an important linen manufacturing town (this fine linen has been traditionally used to make the sleeves of bishops' vestments and as a result it became an allusive term for the job—in 1800 Sydney Smith wrote of "the ermine of the judge or the lawn of the prelate"). **Damask** is from an old form of *Damascus*, where it was first made. The very English **worsted**, a fine woollen cloth, is from *Worstead*, a parish in Norfolk. The linen **holland**, once used for window blinds and covering furniture, is obviously enough from that province of the Netherlands.

Others, now much less well known, similarly reflect places. **Arras**, most familiar now from Shakespeare's *Hamlet* because Polonius hid behind one, only to be killed, was a wall hanging made of a rich tapestry fabric whose name derives from the town of *Arras* in north-east France. Another cotton fabric of the period, **fustian**, is from *Fostat*, a suburb of Cairo. Because fustian was often used for pillows, in the late 1500s it gained the sense of padding and figuratively of pompous speech, in just the same way as *bombast*, mentioned earlier. **Sarsenet** or **sarcenet**, a silk fabric, comes through old French from *Saracen*, an Arab or Muslim of medieval times.

Silk was so expensive that in medieval times only royalty could afford it. In the Elizabethan period the government tried to stop people spending too much money on costly clothes at the expense of more worthy items; what are now called **sumptuary laws** were passed that limited silk to various grades of the nobility. One silk cloth, interwoven with gold threads, was called **baudekin**; this name is from the Italian version, *Baldacco*, of the name of Baghdad. Later, it referred to any rich silk cloth, changed to **baldachin**, and became the word for a ceremonial canopy over an altar or throne, because such canopies were at first covered with the cloth. Another famous medieval silk and gold cloth was called **samite** (you may know Tennyson's *Idylls of the King*: "Clothed in white samite, mystic, wonderful"); this came—much modified—via French and Latin from medieval Greek *hexamiton* (*hexa-*, six + *mitos*, thread, though the experts are still arguing about why).

Such fabrics were generically called **cloth of gold**—the famous meeting near Calais between Henry VIII and Francis I of France in 1520 became known as the **field of the cloth of gold** because of the expensively decorated tents and pavilions that were erected for the occasion. Another was **brocade**, in which the pattern of raised figures was woven in a mixture of silver and gold threads (the name is from Italian *broccato*, from *brocco*, twisted thread; a cheaper version in silk or wool was called **brocatelle**, from Italian *broccatello*, a diminutive of *broccato*; later *brocade* was borrowed for a great range of materials from many fabrics for almost every purpose).

Such fabrics were said in the sixteenth century to be **tinsel** or **tinselled** (from Old French *estincele*, based on Latin *scintilla*, both words meaning a spark), which didn't have today's associations of cheap or tawdry glamour. To **purl** at the same period meant to embroider a fabric with gold or silver thread, with the *purl* being the thread itself; the knitting sense came later.

Ciclatoun (from Persian and Arabic) was a famous medieval fabric; it seems to have died out shortly after Chaucer mentioned it in the *Canterbury Tales* around 1386:

> His robe was of ciclatoun,
> That coste many a jane.

(A *jane* was a small silver coin, named after the city of *Genoa* and also called a *galley-halfpence*, because it was supposed to have been introduced by sailors on the Genoese galleys that traded with London.) Chaucer often drops names for fabrics into his text; another silken one was **sendal**, a thin but rich form of silk whose name is ultimately from Greek *sindōn*, fine linen. In the *Knight's Tale*, he wrote:

> His coat-armour was of a cloth of Tars,
> Couched with pearls white and round and great.

This was expensive, since **cloth of Tars** was an Oriental fabric of great rarity. We aren't sure what it was made from—almost certainly silk—though it has been suggested that it might have been mixed with fine Tibetan goat hair; *Tars* refers to *Tartary*, a medieval region of Asia and eastern Europe. Another costly Eastern silken fabric that might have been a mixture, this time with camel hair, was **camlet** (Arabic *khamlat*, woollen plush), first recorded just after Chaucer's time, but whose name came in later centuries to be applied to fine fabrics of other materials, including one made of angora.

Linen was another fabric widely used, which could be finely woven to make intimate undergarments, or coarsely prepared in lower qualities for other purposes. **Buckram** has gone from one state to the other: in the thirteenth century, it meant a kind of fine linen or cotton cloth (the name is from Old French *boquerant*, perhaps from *Bukhoro* in central Asia, so it's yet another geographically inspired name); by Chaucer's time it was a coarse linen cloth stiffened with glue or starch; later still it turned into a metaphor for men who were stiff in appearance or nature. Chaucer is the first known person to mention **lake**, another fine linen, writing of a man putting on a shirt of "cloth of lake fine and clear"; the word is an ancient Germanic one. A coarser type, though common and widely used for clothing, was called **lockram** (from *Locronan*, a town in Brittany); it can't have been too coarse, because the phrase **lockram-jawed** appears later, meaning having jaws covered with flesh as thin as lockram, so "thin-faced", as it is explained in Captain Grose's *Dictionary of the Vulgar Tongue* in 1811.

Yet another was **osnaburg** (an English version of the name of the North German town *Osnabrück*, another linen-manufacturing centre). An even rougher type of linen called **harden** got its name from the **hards** of flax, the coarser parts separated out during a manufacturing process called **hackling** in which the raw flax was separated from the rubbish with big steel combs. **Linsey** was another coarse linen of Tudor times and its name forms part of **linsey-woolsey**, a mixture of linen and wool fibres, though it later became the name for a much inferior cloth of coarse wool woven on cotton. You can tell its humble status from Elizabeth Gaskell's mention of it in *Sylvia's Lovers* of 1863:

> How well it was, thought the young girl, that she had doffed her bed-gown and linsey-woolsey petticoat, her working-dress, and made herself smart in her stuff gown, when she sat down to work with her mother.

The **stuff** she mentions was a generic name for a woollen fabric lacking a nap or pile, which comes from Old French *estoffe*, material (modern French *étoffe*, fabric or material); Thomas Dyche and William Pardon described it in their dictionary of 1735 as

> Any Sort of Commodity made of Woollen Thread, &c. but in a particular Manner those thin light ones that Women make or line their Gowns of or with.

In *Two Centuries of Costume in America*, which Alice Morse Earle published in 1903, she remarks of the first colonists in New England in the early seventeenth century that they wore

> horseman's coats of tan-colored linsey-woolsey
> or homespun ginger-lyne or brown perpetuana;
> fawn-colored mandillions and deer-colored
> cassocks.

Ginger-lyne was a light sandy-brown colour, like that of ginger, one of the "sad colours" that were favoured by Puritans in the New World at that period; a **mandillion** or **mandilion** was a loose coat or cassock, ultimately from Arabic *mindil* or *mandil* for a sash or turban-cloth. The **perpetuana** she mentions was a woollen fabric; as you may guess from the name, it wore well.

She also mentions several times another woollen fabric called **kersey** (once more from a place, this time the village of *Kersey* in Suffolk), a ribbed and rather coarse narrow cloth that was sold in lengths a yard wide; this distinguished it from **broadcloth**, which was—as its name implies—twice the width. Sir Arthur Conan Doyle included it in his historical novel *Micah Clarke*:

> His tunic was made of coarse sad-coloured kersey
> stuff with flat new gilded brass buttons, beneath
> which was a whitish callamanca vest edged with
> silver.

Callamanca was a kind of glazed woollen cloth with raised stripes of the same colour, whose origin I've been unable to trace. Another cloth of the eighteenth century made from wool was **sagathy**, a lightweight serge, whose name came via French from the Spanish *sagatí*.

A grey woollen cloth in medieval England was called **muster-devillers**; it is said to have originated in the town in Normandy now called Montivilliers and to have got its name from a version of the way the town's name was spelled at the time. Among the arrangements made by the council of the city of York to welcome Richard III on 4 August 1483 were detailed instructions on what to wear. In modern spelling, it ended:

> All others of whatever occupation, dressed in
> blue, violet and musterdevillers, shall meet our
> sovereign lord on foot at St James' church.

The following century a widely used woollen fabric had the name **mockado** (apparently, the *Oxford English Dictionary* says, a corruption of the Italian word *mocajardo* that comes from an Arabic term which has also given us *mohair*). A much finer cloth of the seventeenth and eighteenth centuries, often with a glazed finish, was called **tammy**, though nobody seems to know where that came from.

Sailors demanded cloth that was strong and durable. Canvas, made from linen or hemp (the name is based on the Latin *cannabis* for hemp, but there was no chance of getting high except by climbing the mast), was sometimes used for clothes as well as sails. But the classic maritime clothing fabric was **duck** (Dutch *doek*, linen or linen cloth, a word which is related to German *Tuch*, cloth), in earlier times made from linen but later cotton; there are many references to **duck trousers** in particular, as in *Two Years Before the Mast* by Richard Henry Dana (1840):

> The change from the tight frock-coat, silk cap,
> and kid gloves of an undergraduate at Harvard, to
> the loose duck trousers, checked shirt, and
> tarpaulin hat of a sailor, though somewhat of a
> transformation, was soon made; and I supposed
> that I should pass very well for a Jack tar.

When the weather got especially bad, sailors wore jackets of a stout type of woollen cloth that they dubbed **fearnought**, because the material was also used to protect the doors to the powder magazine; Robert Kerr mentioned it in one volume of his *A General History and Collection of Voyages and Travels* of 1824:

> The poor seamen not only suffered much by the
> cold, but had scarcely ever a dry thread about
> them: I therefore distributed among the crews of
> both the ships, not excepting the officers, two
> bales of a thick woollen stuff, called Fearnought,
> which is provided by the government, so that
> every body on board had now a warm jacket,
> which at this time was found both comfortable
> and salutary.

Another fabric often associated with sailors was **nankeen**, a yellowish cotton cloth likewise mostly used for trousers (the geographical theme of this chapter continues to the end, since its name comes from the Chinese city of *Nanking*).

Wigs on the green

IN THE ELIZABETHAN PERIOD, wigs were worn, but for strictly utilitarian purposes. It was the next century that saw their transformation into items of high fashion.

From James Joyce's *Ulysses* (1922):

> But Tommy said he wanted the ball and Edy told him no that baby was playing with the ball and if he took it there'd be wigs on the green but Tommy said it was his ball and he wanted his ball and he pranced on the ground, if you please. The temper of him!

Originally Irish and eighteenth century, *wigs on the green* meant that a dispute among men was becoming serious enough that it might escalate to fisticuffs, resulting in the participants' wigs landing on the ground. It needs explaining now, when a wig isn't a standard part of a gentleman's costume, but for about a century and a half from the 1660s no man with the slightest concern for his image would have been seen in public without one.

Wigs were brought over to England by Charles II and his

courtiers at the Restoration in 1660, though it was his brother, the Duke of York, who actually led the fashion. It was really all the fault of Louis XIII, who went bald and took to wearing a wig in 1624. In those days royal fancies were immediately copied by those around him and in the 1650s this included the future English king, in exile on the continent.

Samuel Pepys, the rising young naval administrator, was on the *Naseby* with the new king on his journey back from the Netherlands. Pepys was a man of fashion, very aware of new styles. But his diary shows he was undecided for a while about this new headwear idea, disliking the examples he saw. On 3 November 1663 he finally succumbed:

> By and by comes Chapman, the periwigg-maker, and upon my liking it, without more ado I went up, and there he cut off my haire, which went a little to my heart at present to part with it; but, it being over, and my periwigg on, I paid him £3 for it; and away went he with my owne haire to make up another of.

He was clearly unsure of himself, but records the next day,

> Up and to my office, shewing myself to Sir W Batten, and Sir J Minnes, and no great matter made of my periwigg, as I was afeard there would be.

By the 13th of the month he had his second wig, made as he says of his own hair—not that uncommon at the time and later called a **natural wig**.

Periwig, our modern spelling, was then the usual word for it; only later in the century was it abbreviated by men in a hurry. The French original, then as now, was *perruque* (from Italian *perrucca*, perhaps ultimately from Latin *pilus*, hair); a century earlier it had been imported into English and respelled as **peruke**. Its original sense was the same as the first French one: a natural head of hair. At first a wig was called a **false peruke** or **artificial peruke**. In 1613 the historian and lawyer Sir John Hayward wrote,

> When their owne hair failed, they set artificiall
> Peruques, with long locks upon their heades.

By the process called folk etymology, in which people alter strange foreign words to make them more acceptable and sensible-sounding, *peruke* became *periwig*. It's not so extraordinary a shift as it seems: there were several stages in it through the sixteenth century, starting with *perwyke*, in which the *u* of the French was altered to *w*; the final form emerged via *perewyke* and *perewick*. Though an oddity of recording, the form *perwyke* is known rather earlier than *peruke*, since it appears in Henry VIII's accounts in 1529 against the cost of a wig for Sexten, the king's jester or fool.

Charles II wore what became known as a **full-bottomed wig**, which had three masses of curls, two in front of the shoulders and one hanging down the back. This became the dress fashion until the early eighteenth century. It gave a man stature but was inconvenient for all but formal occasions. After it went out of fashion, the style was retained by lawyers and is preserved in the headwear of senior British judges. Because by the latter part of the eighteenth century only the most eminent continued to wear them at any time, they became derisively known as **bigwigs**.

To ease the inconvenience of these wigs, men pulled the hair back and enclosed it in a taffeta bag at the back of the head, making a **bag-wig**. Benjamin Franklin wrote from Paris in 1767, having dressed in French fashion for the first time:

> Only think what a Figure I make in a little Bag Wig and naked Ears!

Tobias Smollett mentioned a variant of the style in *Sir Launcelot Greaves* of 1760:

> He wore upon his head a bag-wig, à la pigeon, made by an old acquaintance in Wapping.

The **pigeon-wig**, one with **pigeon-wings**, had the side hairs dressed up. A variant of the bag-wig was the **tie-wig**, in which the hair was instead tied with a knot of ribbon. These were often very large: Horace Walpole wrote in a letter to Sir Horace Mann in 1745:

> I could have no hope of getting at his ear, for he has put on such a first-rate tie-wig, on his

> admission to the admiralty board, that nothing
> without the lungs of a boatswain can ever think
> to penetrate the thickness of the curls.

After the battle of Ramillies in 1706, a wig called the **ramilie** came into fashion for a while; it had a long plait behind, tied with a big bow at the top and a smaller one at the bottom. The **club-wig** or **Cadogan** (supposedly named after the First Earl Cadogan), a simple wig that was popular with both men and women at the end of the eighteenth century, had a pigtail with a bulge at the end (hence like a club) that was tied with a narrow ribbon.

In the eighteenth century, styles multiplied, every class or profession seeming to develop one of their own. A clergyman of Queen Anne's time might wear a **cauliflower wig**, while army officers had the **brigadier** (tied back in two curls; tied in just one curl it was a **major**). Because King George III preferred one the colour of his own brown hair, that kind became known as a **brown George** (which had previously been the name for the daily loaf of bread issued to the infantry soldier, another name for which was **ammunition loaf**). A further wig of the time, rough-cropped and military, featured in Thackeray's *Vanity Fair*:

> Her lord ... was a withered, old, lean man in a
> greatcoat and a **Brutus wig**, slinking about Gray's
> Inn of mornings chiefly and dining alone at clubs.

Yet another was the **buzz-wig**, a large bushy type.

There were many more: the **comet**, the **caxon** (supposedly named after the man who made it, though nobody knows more), the **negligent**, the **Adonis**, the **chancellor**, the **Dalmahoy** (worn by tradesmen), and the **Chedreux** (which appears in *London Pride: or When the World was Younger*, by M E Braddon, dated 1896: "I was wearing a Chedreux peruke that ought to strike 'em dead"). Tradesmen of the better sort tended towards the **bob-wig**, one in which the bottom locks were turned up into short curls called *bobs*, or the **scratch wig**, a small, short wig ("They were all stout ill-favoured men," wrote Harrison Ainsworth in his novel *Jack Sheppard*, "attired in the regular jail-livery of scratch wig and snuff-coloured suit"); it was sometimes colloquially called a **natty scratch**. Another slangy term for a wig from the end of the eighteenth century was **jasey**, possibly derived from *jersey*, especially applied to a wig made of worsted. Thackeray uses it in his *Burlesques*:

> "Hadn't you better settle your wig?" says I,
> offering it to him on the tip of my cane, "and we'll
> arrange time and place when you have put your
> jasey in order."

It was standard for the wig to be sprinkled with **hair-powder**, basically flour scented with substances such as orange flower, lavender, or orris root, so men spoke of **flouring** their wigs. It was often inconvenient, as was recorded by Nathaniel Hawthorne in *Sights From a Steeple*:

> I discern the rich old merchant, putting himself
> to the top of his speed, lest the rain should
> convert his hair-powder to a paste. Unhappy
> gentleman!

One of the reasons for the demise of the wig in British daily life was the tax that Pitt's government put on hair-powder in 1795, one guinea per year. This was regarded as quite beyond sufferance, so powdering died, and with it the fashion for wigs.

Incidentally, the once-famous British political party called the **Whigs**, the forerunners of the Liberal Democrats, had nothing to do with wigs. Their name is from the Scots word *whiggamore*, a nickname of seventeenth-century Scottish rebels, which is said to have been a derogatory term for mounted Scottish cattle drovers (it's from *whig*, to drive or spur on, and *mare*, a female horse).

Get ahead, get a hat

HATS, OF COURSE, have been around for as long as people have worn clothes. At a time in which wearing them is less common than in any recent century, their names are becoming markers of history.

In 1965 the British Hat Council felt it necessary because of declining sales to create the advertising slogan of my chapter heading. Earlier generations would have found the advice otiose, since only the meanest members of society went about without one. Photographs from the early to middle twentieth century immediately strike us because of all the hats, whether it's a sea of flat caps at a football match, a hoard of be-bowlered city clerks crossing London Bridge on their way to work, a group of heavily hatted women enjoying a walk in the park, or any man in an old black-and-white film, whose head is invariably topped off with a Homburg, trilby, fedora, or other style.

The soft hat called a **Homburg** came from the exclusive German spa town of Bad Homburg near Frankfurt, often frequented by royalty in late Victorian times. The hat became fashionable in London because the Prince of Wales (later Edward VII) regularly visited the town from 1882 onwards, liked the style of the local hat and brought it home with him (in 1893, advertisers in American newspapers were calling it "the latest fad", though they spelled it *Homberg*). In the 1930s it became known as the **Anthony Eden**, or the **Eden** hat, after the then foreign secretary.

The other two of the three classic styles of men's headwear of the period were actually popularized by actresses. The **fedora**, later to be the classic topping of the Italian-American mobster, was named after the title and main character in a famous play by the French playwright Victorien Sardou, first performed in 1882 with Sarah Bernhardt as the hat-wearing Russian princess Fédora Romanov. The name of the **trilby** comes from a play adapted by the American Paul Potter from a book by George du Maurier. The latter had been an immense hit when it came out in 1894, as a writer in the *New York Tribune* in March 1895 wailed:

> We are beset by a veritable epidemic of Trilby fads. Trilby bonnets and gowns and shoes, Trilby accents of speech and Trilby poses of person. Trilby tableaux, teas and dances. Trilby ice cream and Trilby sermons, Trilby clubs and reading classes and prize examinations, Trilby nomenclature for everybody and everything.

The play was brought over to London in November 1895 by the impresario Beerbohm Tree and was a huge success, ensuring that the hat worn by the bare-footed, chain-smoking, 20-year-old leading lady Dorothea Baird would become part of the British trilby craze. Her picture, wearing that hat, appeared on postcards, in advertisements, on chocolate boxes, and in newspapers.

Women's hats of the period also had names with literary associations. The **Dolly Varden** was large, with one side bent down, "abundantly trimmed with flowers" as the *Oxford English Dictionary* puts it. The name came from the coquettish character in Charles Dickens's *Barnaby Rudge*. The fashion for it started about 1872, but it was not universally popular, it would seem, to judge from a snooty comment in *The Athens Messenger* (the one in Ohio) in May that year:

> The maids of Athens, and the matrons too, do not take to Dolly Vardens worth a cent.

In the same month, *Harper's Weekly* commented,

> Was ever any new costume more criticized than the new 'Dolly Varden'.

Another a little later was the **Merry Widow**, an ornate and widebrimmed hat whose style and name derived from the hat worn by Lily Elsie in the London premiere of Franz Lehar's operetta in June 1907. The show made Ms Elsie a star and the focus of a craze, just as happened with Dorothea Baird a decade earlier.

Her picture—wearing that hat, of course—appeared very widely in advertisements and picture postcards. This style was as common in the US as in Britain; Wu Tingfang wrote in confusion in his book *America Through the Spectacles of an Oriental Diplomat* in 1914:

> There you will see women wearing 'Merry Widow' hats who are not widows but spinsters, or married women whose husbands are very much alive, and the hats in many cases are as large as three feet in diameter.

He was right about their size. Some American examples became so large, in fact, that a postcard of the time featured a wearer staring sadly at a sign by a lift:

> Ladies with Merry Widow Hats Take Freight Elevator.

Another style, popularized by the Prince of Wales in 1896, was the **boater**, a straw hat with a flat crown and brim, so named because it became the usual informal wear when messing about in boats, but now remembered by many people mostly as part of the official costume of their local butcher, not least Corporal "They don't like it up 'em" Jones of *Dad's Army*.

The formal men's hat of the nineteenth century was the **top hat**, an updated version of a hat faced with beaver fur of earlier centuries, though by the 1830s silk ones became standard. Tall and round, with the brim curling up at the sides, it's familiar still from costume dramas and very formal wear. Colloquially in Britain it was a **topper**; in the US a **plug-hat**, perhaps because the head fitted it like a plug in a pipe. An older version was called the **bell-topper**, **beltopper**, or **belltopper** because it had a bell-shaped crown; in 1889 Edward Wakefield wrote in *New Zealand After Fifty Years*:

> Gentlepeople, whether in town or country, dress
> almost exactly as they do in England, except that
> the beltopper hat is comparatively seldom seen.

A variety of the top hat was the **crush hat** or **opera hat**, whose crown could be collapsed for convenience during a visit to the theatre; it was often called a **gibus**, after Antoine Gibus, the Frenchman who around 1812 designed one of cloth on a metal frame. William Makepeace Thackeray wrote of one wearer in *The Book of Snobs* of 1847:

> Ask little Tom Prig, who is there in all his glory,
> knows everybody, has a story about every one;
> and, as he trips home to his lodgings in Jermyn
> Street, with his gibus-hat and his little glazed
> pumps, thinks he is the fashionablest young
> fellow in town, and that he really has passed a
> night of exquisite enjoyment.

Another slangy British term for the taller varieties of top hat was **chimney-pot hat** (**stove-pipe hat** in the US) which Jerome K Jerome mentioned in *Idle Thoughts of an Idle Fellow* in 1886:

> His first half-hour is occupied in trying to decide
> whether to wear his light suit with a cane and
> drab billycock, or his black tails with a chimney-
> pot hat and his new umbrella.

The **wide-awake** was a soft felt hat with a broad brim and a low crown, said to have been jocularly named because it had no nap. It's mentioned in *Scouting for Boys* by Robert Baden-Powell of 1908 and also in *The British Workman Past and Present* by The Reverend M C F Morris of 1928:

> And lastly there was the wagoner himself, a lad,
> say, of eighteen summers, a fine, strong,
> healthy-looking young fellow, well clad, and
> wearing on his head a 'raddidoo' or wide-awake
> hat, with perhaps a peacock's feather or some
> other embellishment at the side.

(**Raddidoo** defeats me completely.)

The **billycock** was a hard, round hat. Etymologically, it has been a matter of contention, with many references saying firmly that it's from the name of William Coke of Norfolk, who commissioned its manufacture (so *billy-coke* or *billy-cock*, though his family name was actually pronounced "cook"). Not so. The name is actually from a style of the early eighteenth century called a **bully-cock**. The original *bullies* were upper-class sporting gangs of the period, who became a terror on the streets and gave their name to intimidating the vulnerable. (There's another level of word-historical curiosity here, since *bully* is from Dutch *boele*,

GET AHEAD, GET A HAT ·

lover, and was at first a term of endearment applied to either sex. Later it became a way to address a male friend, hence the name for the group.) A bully-cock was a bully's hat whose brim was *cocked*, or turned up. In Andrew Lang's 1880 book of anecdotes about Oxford, he records a 1727 description of an Oxford "smart" of that time:

> He is easily distinguished by a stiff silk gown ... a
> broad bully-cock'd hat, or a square cap of about
> twice the usual size; white stockings; thin
> Spanish leather shoes. His clothes lined with
> tawdry silk, and his shirt ruffled down the bosom
> as well as at the wrists.

William Coke was responsible for a very similar hat, which is part of the reason for the confusion. But his was what we now call the **bowler**. He had it made by the makers Lock of London in 1850 as a hard hat to protect the heads of his gamekeepers when out riding and chasing poachers. It was made of felt hardened with shellac. Mr Coke reputedly tested the prototype by jumping on it, an abuse it survived undented. It ought to be called a **Coke hat**, which indeed it was for a while, or perhaps a Lock hat. But Messrs Lock had it manufactured by the firm of Thomas and William Bowler and their name has stuck to it, no doubt because a hat with a crown like a bowl *ought* to be called a bowler. In the US, the usual name was and is **derby**, after the Epsom Derby (though said differently), partly because of its riding associations, but mainly because the hat had by the latter part of the century become standard wear for the many Londoners for whom Derby Day was a de facto public holiday.

A **cocked hat** was any kind that had the brim permanently turned up. These had been much in fashion in the eighteenth century, especially the three-cornered hat worn both by civilians and by army and navy officers. In the nineteenth century, only after it had gone out of fashion in favour of the beaver hat, this came to be called a **tricorn** or **tricorne** hat. Towards the end of the eighteenth century a type cocked only at front and back became common. By analogy, modern fashion historians call this a **bicorne**, though likewise the term doesn't seem to have been used by its wearers. Naval officers kept the bicorne, though around the time of Nelson they turned it ninety degrees to point front and back instead of side to side.

Let's take the story back a lot further, to the medieval period. A female head-covering called the **wimple** (a Germanic word, related to modern German *Wimpel*, pennon or streamer), a cloth headdress covering the head, neck, and the sides of the face, is still familiar to many of us today because it forms part of the traditional costume of nuns. Another medieval headdress for women was called the **barbette** (strangely, the word seems to be from French *barbe*, beard). It was supposedly Eleanor of Aquitaine who was responsible for introducing it to England in the eleventh century. It consisted of a piece of fabric folded over the head and under the chin. In later times, the hair under it was enclosed in a **crespine** or **crespinette** (from an Old French word that's the source of modern *crêpe*, from Latin *crispa*, curled), or **caul**, a decorated hairnet of gold or silver thread or silk lace. Another headdress of the medieval period was the **couvrechef** (Old French, a head covering) or **coverchief**, the Anglicized version that had been converted by common usage into a form that seemed to make more sense, from which came the yet further modified *kerchief* (the *handkerchief* came along in the sixteenth century).

At the time of the Norman Conquest and for several centuries afterwards, men went bare-headed or wore a conical cap that modern writers call the **Phrygian cap**, because it was similar to one worn by the Phrygians of Asia Minor and which was given to a slave in Roman times when he gained his freedom; for this reason, in the seventeenth century it became known as the **cap of liberty**. In the thirteenth century, men sometimes wore a white linen band under it—rather like the women's barbette—called a **coif**. In bad weather men wore a hood or cowl with a cape called a **gorget** (Old French *gorgete*, from *gorge*, throat) covering the shoulders. In later years this was **dagged**, cut into deep scallops (the word may be related to *tag*, though nobody knows for sure).

By the late thirteenth century, the point of the hood had become lengthened into a long tube. This was the **liripipe** (medieval Latin *liripipium*, which has been variously and curiously explained as the tippet of a hood, a cord, a shoelace, and the inner sole-leather of shoes). This was also part of academic costume, and a few American universities still use the word for the tails of their graduates' ceremonial hoods. The liripipe was often several feet long, so long that it had to be carried over the arm or wound around the head as a sort of turban to avoid tripping on it. By the time of Henry VI, this had been converted into a hat called a **chaperon** (the French word for a hood) which survives as part of the formal garb of Knights of the Garter. *Chaperon* here is the same word as modern *chaperone* for an older woman who protects the virtue of young women at social events; it seems to derive from the joking idea that the chaperone protects the girl as the hood did the head.

By the fifteenth century, high-crowned hats had become more common, one type having a name that appeared in a dozen different forms but which is now often written in costume histories as **copintank**; it might be from Latin *caputium*, head-covering. One variation is **capotaine**, which Sir Walter Scott used in his historical novel *Kenilworth* of 1821:

> She laid aside her travelling cloak and capotaine
> hat, and placed them beside her, so that she
> could assume them in an instant.

A similarly-shaped hat of the Tudor and Stuart periods was called a **sugar loaf**, because it resembled the usual conical shape of a block of refined sugar.

Also in the fifteenth century appeared the hat that has become notorious as an example of how words can be altered by mistakes that are then copied. This was the **bycoket** (brought over from Old French *bicoque*, the same word as old Italian *bicocca*, a little castle on a hill, because the hat had a high crown). Through a misprint in Edward Hall's *Chronicle of Edward IV* in 1548, in which *bycocket* was written as *abococket*, which was then copied by others and modified, it ended up as **abacot**, a word you'll find in some older works on fashion and in some old dictionaries (Noah Webster defined it as "the cap of state formerly used by English kings, wrought into the figure of two crowns"). William S Walsh wrote in his *Handy-Book of Literary Curiosities* of 1904:

> It has been handed down to our time,—a standing exemplar of the solidarity of dictionaries, and of the ponderous indolence with which philologers repeat without examining the errors of their predecessors.

That's not a trap that today's dictionary-makers would fall into, of course.

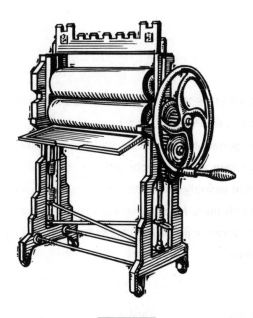

PART 5

Names, Employment, & Communications

What's in a name?

SURNAMES WERE UNCOMMON in Britain before the thirteenth century. As the population grew, it became important for tax or legal reasons to be able to distinguish between all the people with the same name—which John out of possibly half a dozen in a village was the one behind with his taxes, for example. As a result, surnames started with the wealthy or propertied classes and slowly worked down to everyone.

Some names came from the place where a person lived (**Lincoln, Washington**), from one's father's name (**McDonald, Robertson**), from some personal foible or characteristic (**White, Little**), or from the job one did. Some of those occupations are still recognizable: **Smith** is the common one for a worker in metal, but **Archer, Baker, Butcher, Carter, Cook, Glover, Miller,** and **Potter** are also among those that pose no problem for us. Many others, though, preserve references to working lives that are outdated or alien.

A man named **Badger**, for example, had nothing to do with the animal (who was called *brock* in ancient times) but would have been a pedlar (who carried his wares about with him in a bag—originally he was a *bagger*) or who acted as a middleman, buying up corn, fish, butter and cheese and selling them on; badgers were unpopular because they were believed to manipulate prices for their own benefit. A **Chapman** was in much the same line, being a trader or pedlar; it's from Old English *céap*, bargaining or trade, which also appears in the London street name *Cheapside*. So was a **Copeman**, whose name is from the Old Norse equivalent of *céap*. Obviously enough, a **Packman** was a pedlar, too. Less obviously so was a **Jagger**, whose name derives from a Yorkshire dialect word for a pedlar, whose origin is *jag*, a pack. Upton Sinclair used the word in *Love's Pilgrimage* (1911):

> The next day he was up at dawn, constructing
> tables and stands; and later on he hired the
> farmer's 'jagger-wagon', and drove in for Corydon
> and Cedric and the trunks.

A **Tranter** might in various places be a man who let his horse and cart out on hire (it might be from Latin *transvehere*, to convey); however, it often specifically meant a trader or middleman—George Mason noted in his 1801 work with the modest title *A Supplement to Johnson's English Dictionary: of which the palpable errors are attempted to be rectified, and its material omissions supplied*:

> Country people, amongst whom alone this word is
> current, extend its meaning to all those who
> purchase any kind of provisions in order to sell
> them again.

A man who drove pack-horses might once have been called **Sumpter** (from Latin *sagmatis*, pack saddle), a name which was later applied to the pack animal itself, as in Sir Arthur Conan Doyle's *The White Company* of 1891:

> After them came twenty-seven sumpter horses
> carrying tent-poles, cloth, spare arms, spurs,
> wedges, cooking kettles, horse-shoes, bags of
> nails and the hundred other things which
> experience had shown to be needful in a harried
> and hostile country.

The original **Mercers** were also dealers, but in costly fabrics such as silk or velvet (the word comes from French *mercier*, based on Latin *merx*, goods, which also gave us *merchant, market, and mercantile*). There's no doubt that a **Spicer** was once a seller of spices, but he might also have prepared or sold medicines and drugs. A **Chandler** was originally a maker and seller specifically of candles (from Old French *chandelle*, candle) or he might have been the man who superintended the supply of candles, an expensive commodity, in a large household; the modern sense of a dealer in groceries and provisions arrived later.

However, some medieval **Hawker** must have been a keeper of hawks, not a travelling seller of goods, a sense that came along only in the sixteenth century (**Faulkner** is related, being a variant spelling of *falconer*). An ancestor of someone named **Pinner** or **Pinder** might have had the job of rounding up stray animals and putting them in the local pound or pinfold (Middle English *pinder*, to shut up). His name appears in the title of the ancient and anonymous Robin Hood ballad, *The Jolly Pinder of Wakefield*:

> "There is neither knight nor squire," said the
> pinder,
> "Nor barron that is so bold,
> Dare make a trespasse to the town of Wakefield,
> But his pledge goes to the pinfold."

If animals escaped from the common land into enclosed areas such as woodland, it would have been the fault of the **Hayward**, the officer in charge of the fences and enclosures in a parish (*ward* here is in the sense of guarding). The surnames **Hoggard** or **Hoggart** would once have been written *hogherd*, the name for a man who looks after pigs, a swineherd. In medieval times a *park* was an enclosed tract of land in which wild animals were kept for hunting; some ancestral **Parker** would have been its gamekeeper; **Woodward** commemorates a person managing an area of woodland or forest, a **Forester**. A **Granger** or **Grainger** was a farm bailiff at this period, whose job was to collect the local produce taken as rent in kind and store it in the barns of the lord of the manor, at his *grange*.

A more arcane occupation was that of **Cheater**, short for *escheator*; his job was to supervise the reversion of property to his feudal lord in the absence of legal heirs (the word comes from *eschete*, a lot or portion; there were so many opportunities for unfair dealing that *cheat* came to have our modern meaning). Someone called **Dempster** would have had a forebear who was a judge of minor disputes; the term comes from Old English *dēmian*, to judge; though not so common in England, every Scottish laird down to the eighteenth century would have had a dempster for this purpose. Another official job now defunct was that of **Conner**. It's from *cun(nen)*, to examine or test; it appears most often in the compound *ale-conner* which is mentioned on page 229.

Other old surname-occupations were concerned with warfare. Someone with the name of **Quarrell** may once have been a maker of crossbow bolts; they were called *quarrels*—from Latin *quadrus*, square—because they typically had square heads. A **Bowman** was, obviously enough, an archer, as a **Bowyer** might also be, though he was more usually a maker and seller of longbows. An ancestral **Fletcher** specifically made and sold arrows (Old French *flechier*, from *fleche*, arrow). Such words often turn up in modern swords and sorcery novels, as here in *Stone of Tears* by Terry Goodkind:

> We need to kill their arrow makers and fletchers,
> bowyers and blacksmiths, all the craftsmen who
> can make and repair bows, arrows, and other

> weapons. They will have sacks of goose wings
> for fletching arrows. They must be stolen or
> burned.

Naylor is merely a disguised spelling of *nailer*, a man who made nails, while one who constructed wooden chests might have been given the name **Arkwright** (borrowed through French from Latin *arca*, chest, a word we're familiar with from phrases like *Ark of the Covenant* and *Noah's ark*). A man called **Lorimer** (from Latin *lōrum*, harness or strap) took his surname from his trade of making spurs and other metal items for horse harness, as did a forebear of someone named **Spurrier**.

A **Webster** was a weaver (one, etymologically speaking, who wove webs, from Old English *webb*, hence the related surname **Webb**); websters were originally female, though that distinction was lost very early on, in the same way that in medieval times **Baxter** was the name given to a female baker. Also associated with the staple English medieval manufacture of woollen cloth was some ancestral **Fuller**, who *fulled* freshly woven cloth by beating and trampling it in a slurry of clay and water called *fuller's earth* to scour and thicken it. A **Tucker** might also have been a fuller, in the West Country in particular, but they often took on a later stage in the process—dressing the cloth and stretching it on frames to dry (it's probably from an old Germanic word *tucken*, to draw or pull sharply).

Surprisingly, a **Lavender** had nothing to do with the plant, but was a man who cleaned woollen cloth (it's ultimately from Latin *lavare*, to wash; our modern *launder* and *laundry* are variations), though an ancestor might instead have been a washerwoman. A **Challenor** or **Chaloner** forebear made *chalons*, blankets or bed covers (possibly from the French town *Châlons-sur-Marne*). A man called **Bleacher** would have been responsible for bleaching newly woven cloth and a colleague who then dyed it might be called a **Lister** (from Old Norse *lita*, to dye).

Some other surnames that disguise old occupations include **Kellogg**, a pork butcher (from *kullen*, to kill + *hog*), an early **Kemp** was probably a successful jouster or wrestler (from Old English *cempa*, warrior), a **Bunter** was a sifter of flour (from Middle English *bont(en)*, to sieve), someone named **Latimer** would have been a clerk or keeper of records in Latin (from Anglo-Norman French *latinier*) and a **Striker** may well have been a man whose job was to ensure that measures of corn were accurate by passing a flat stick over the brim of the measure to level its contents—a name which comes from a Middle English word *strike*, meaning to stroke.

Obscure
occupations

MOST OF THESE OCCUPATIONS are at least under-
standable to us today, even though few of us come
into contact with them, let alone engage in them.
But the multiplicity of named jobs spawned by the Industrial
Revolution often defeated even the experts.

When the first census was taken in England and Wales in 1801,
about 35% of the working population were occupied on the
land. By 1921 this had dropped to less than 10%, a decline coun-
terbalanced by rises in those employed in new jobs in manufacturing and commerce. A half century earlier, a report on
the 1871 census noted "How remarkably every branch of industry is shooting out in new directions and giving rise to new
employments".

It was often unclear from their titles exactly what some workers in these new employments actually did, a problem that you

may feel recurs in some white-collar office jobs today. The 1881 census report listed a set of 100 jobs with the comment that these were "all names of occupations in current use, and yet such that in all probability an ordinary educated man would know at most but one or two of them, and often would not know a single one". If they were unclear then, they're even more obscure now.

As an example of what baffled Victorian census-takers, the list included the job of **branner**; he worked in the tinplate industry, which coated thin sheet iron with tin to make the raw material for tin cans. He worked the **branning machine**, which cleaned protective palm oil from tinned plate by means of revolving brushes covered with bran, hence the name. As an example of the extreme subdivision of labour, how about the job of **nutter**, also called a **nutter-up** or **buttoner-up**; this man had the specific and surely mind-numbing job of screwing finished nuts on to the end of their companion bolts so they could be sold as one item.

In the case of a **maidenmaker**, there was some excuse for Victorian educated ignorance, since *maiden* was a northern dialect term for what the rest of England called a *dolly* (or which some Yorkshire and Lancashire people knew as a *peggy*), a short pole with a ring of wooden pegs on the end that was used to agitate wet clothes in the washing tub (the census list called this device a *washing-machine*, showing once again how meaning can change even when the words stay the same, as these devices were operated entirely by human muscle). While we're considering mildly risqué-sounding occupations, how about **faggoter**, another in the list. This comes from *faggot* (ultimately from Greek *phakelos*, bundle), a bundle of small branches or sticks bound together, usually for fuel—**fire and faggot** was once a reference to burning heretics at the stake. In this case a faggoter had the job of bundling together not wood but lengths of scrap metal, ready to be melted down and reused. One who worked with wood faggots was called a **faggot maker**; a related job was **bavin maker**, where a *bavin* (source unknown) was a smaller version of the faggot, made with brushwood and intended to heat bakers' ovens. And what of **doctor maker**? That makes no sense until you learn that the metal scrapers for removing excess colour from the rollers of nineteenth-century calico printing machines were called *doctors*. As the equivalent devices in modern colour printing machines have the same name, specialist firms still make doctors, but it's doubtful that there's anyone with that job title on the premises.

Other obscure trades from the 1881 list included **sprigger**, an embroiderer who specialized in working designs of sprigs, usually in the form of flowers and leaves; **spragger**, a man who inserted "lockers, scotches, sprags, or snibbles" (short billets of wood, the origins of whose names are all about equally obscure) into the wheels of a railway vehicle or mine tram to prevent its moving; **beatster** (from *beet*, an Old English word meaning to repair or make good), a mender of fishing nets by hand with twine and shuttle; **gambrel maker**, who split and sawed timber to make hooks on which to suspend carcasses in butchers' shops (*gambrel* is from Old Northern French *gambier*, a forked stick, from *gambe*, leg); and **willyer**, who operated a **willeying machine** (from an Old English word that's also the source of our *willow* and *withy*, because early examples of such machines were made like baskets) which separated the matted fibres of raw wool, cotton, or flax and cleaned out dirt and foreign matter.

A couple of the terms in the 1881 list of obscure occupations might not have been understood because they were slang. A **horse marine** is described as a lad in charge of a horse that towed a canal barge. The *horse marines* were a mythical body of men. Since for a cavalryman to have his horse on board ship was spectacularly useless, the term was used sarcastically to describe a person out of his element, a landlubber, a bungler, or somebody who rode extremely badly. (Herman Melville noted in *White Jacket* that "To call a man a 'horse-marine,' is, among seamen, one of the greatest terms of contempt.") Another in the list was **idle back maker**, a term for a pottery mould maker, who made them by pouring plaster of Paris into formers called *oases* and allowing it to set. We must assume that this was regarded as easy work, since an **idle-back** was an indolent or lazy person.

In 1927 the then Ministry of Labour produced the *Dictionary of Occupational Terms*, an astonishingly detailed classification of such occupations that its staff had gleaned from nineteenth and early twentieth-century census data. It listed in minutely subdivided detail nearly 17,000 occupations (and that left out the professions and white-collar jobs). It was the Industrial Revolution that had brought many of these jobs into being; mechanization and the loss of heavy manufacturing and labour-intensive farm work in the past century has meant that many of these jobs no longer exist.

There are now few **swineherds** gainfully employed in herding pigs; also defunct are **rick thatchers**, who once constructed the protective waterproof roofs on hay or straw ricks in farmers' fields. New machines have long since rendered redundant the employments of **steam plough attendant**, **threshing machine attendant**, and **traction engine driver**. Equally, there are now few **dairymaids**, since hardly anybody processes milk into butter or cheese on the farm (**milkmaids** must have been in short supply even in the 1920s, since they aren't listed). **Cottager**, in the classifiers' sense of "a farm labourer who lives in a cottage on the farm and does general work on the farm" is also a defunct type of working man. Another term now gone is that of **onehanded man** or **freehanded man**, for an agricultural worker who undertook tasks on contract such as planting, weeding, or hoeing (a person one might now call a *freelance* or *freelancer*, who was originally a medieval mercenary who hired out himself and his lance).

Pottery kilns were once heated by coal or coke and the freshly-made pots had to be protected from fumes by putting them into fireclay boxes called **saggars** (sometimes **saggers**), a word that may be a contraction of *safeguard*. Every large works had its **saggar-makers**. These men had assistants, **saggar-maker's bottom knockers**, whose job was to make the heavy flat bases, beating the fireclay into shape inside an iron hoop using a heavy mallet. Related jobs include the **bedders** and **flinters** who filled the saggars with pottery (the latter using pieces of flint to hold the items in place) and the **kilnman** or **gormer** (presumably from *gorm* or *gaum*, to smear with a sticky substance) who packed the kiln with filled saggars. All vanished when the kilns began to be heated by clean gas or electricity and saggars were no longer needed.

The **burrgrailer** removed burrs from the teeth of combs using a *grail* or *grele*, a type of file (from French *grêler*, to make slender). A **fenter** cut away *fents* from the ends of a piece of woven cloth; these were originally short slits or openings in a robe (from French *fente*, based on Latin *findere*, to split) but later became a term for an unwanted remnant. A **flong maker** worked in the printing industry, because *flongs* (an Anglicized pronunciation of French *flan*, a round cake, the source of our comestible) were glue-impregnated paper sheets used to create an impression of a page of metal type so copies could be cast. In the name of the **malaxerman**, who mixed fireclay for various purposes in a glass-works, appeared the otherwise long obsolete verb *malax*, to knead (French *malaxer*); one rare appearance is in *The Adventures of Ferdinand Count Fathom*, by Tobias Smollett, dated 1753:

> The major, who complained that his appetite had forsaken him, amused himself with some forty hard eggs, malaxed with salt butter.

In the music halls of the nineteenth century, one job of a **greencoat** was to change the numbers at the side of the stage to indicate the next item on the programme; George Augustus Sala notes him dismissively in his *Twice Round the Clock* of 1859 as

> the cotton-stockinged 'greencoat' of the minor theatres.

Also front of house would have been the **limelight operator**, where the *limelight* was the intense white light created by heating a piece of lime in an oxyhydrogen flame, though now it's purely a figurative term for being the focus of public attention. On stage there would probably at some point have been an **equilibrist** (a direct borrowing from French *équilibriste*), a rope-walker or acrobat who exhibited skills in balancing objects; these were often street performers, as Hugh Walpole recorded in *The Fortress* in 1932:

> [While] waiting outside the station for their
> luggage to be brought to them ... an 'equilibrist'
> spun plates high in air, balanced burning paper-
> bags on his chin, and caught cannon-balls in a
> cup on the top of his head.

Also listed is the actorly occupation of **pantomimist**, in its original sense of one who performs in mime or dumb-show.

While we're on recreation, there are now no **billiard markers** around, not least because few people play billiards and have no need of a man-of-all-work to mark up their scores for them in billiard halls and generally look after the players and tables. This was not the acme of occupations, as we can tell from *Madame Midas*, by Fergus Hume (1888):

> Villiers, deserted by all his acquaintances, sank
> lower and lower in the social scale, and the once
> brilliant butterfly of fashion became a billiard
> marker, then a tout at races, and finally a bar
> loafer with no visible means of support.

The business of **bookmaker's runner** or **bookie's runner** was never a proper trade anyway—it had been illegal since 1853 to place cash bets with a bookmaker away from a racecourse, though thousands of people regularly did so with runners in factories and pubs. The job vanished when betting shops became legal in 1961.

At the seaside, there were once many **bathing-machine attendants**, in charge of small sheds on wheels. Persons desiring a bathe would change into their costumes inside and the machine would then be pushed into the sea by human or horse power. They were ugly contraptions. In *The Hunting of the Snark* Lewis Carroll lists the ways by which one may identify a snark:

> The fourth is its fondness for bathing-machines,
> Which it constantly carries about,
> And believes that they add to the beauty of
> scenes—
> A sentiment open to doubt.

And finally, one job in the *Dictionary of Occupational Terms* that has vanished in very recent times is that of **lighthouse keeper**. Automation has made them obsolete; the last lighthouse keepers in the British Isles left their posts at North Foreland in Kent on 26 November 1998.

The long and the short of it

THESE DAYS, whatever their occupation, most people use the metric system of kilograms, metres, and litres. Those few of us still clinging to yards and gallons are using vocabulary that's slowly vanishing from daily life. But once there was a bewildering set of ways to measure things.

In *Tell England*, by Ernest Raymond, dated 1922, the housemaster of Bramhall House in the public school Kensingtowe is having troubles:

> Fillet was in the worst of tempers, having been just incensed by a boy who had declared that two gills equalled one pint, two pints one quart, and two quarts one rod, pole, or perch.

My friends and I at school (rather more recently than 1922) found that last unit oddly intriguing. "Rod, pole, or perch", indeed. Why should one unit have three names? And what was a perch beyond something a caged bird sat on?

Perch is actually from Latin *pertica*, a pole or measuring-rod—it's also the source of the birdcage sense, plus several others. We didn't know it then, and probably wouldn't have cared if we were told, that the measure dates from Anglo-Saxon England (though it wasn't called that then—the word isn't recorded until the fourteenth century) and was 16½ feet or 5½ yards. **Pole** and **rod** were alternative names that came along in the fifteenth century and somehow survived alongside *perch*.

Forty of them—whatever you called them—made a furlong, once a common way to measure land, though nowadays it's limited by law to horse racing. A **furlong** was the length of a furrow in the common fields of a village (it literally means *furrow-long*). Once the ploughman and his ox team had tilled an area one furlong by four perches he was considered to have done his day's work. In *The Tempest*, William Shakespeare has Gonzalo lament,

> Now would I give a thousand furlongs of sea for
> an acre of barren ground.

His **acre** is that ploughman's daily task, taken from an ancient Indo-European term for a field that became Sanskrit *ajra*, Latin *ager*, and Greek *agros* long before it ever reached English.

To measure larger areas in medieval England, the **virgate** of about 30 acres was useful (it's from medieval Latin *virgāta (terræ)*, roughly "yard-land", from Latin *virga*, rod). An even bigger unit before the Norman Conquest was the **hide** of four virgates, about 120 acres, the area it was considered possible for an eight-oxen team to plough in one year and which was enough to support one family (it's an Anglo-Saxon word linked to *household*). After the Conquest it was replaced by the **carucate**, a highly variable unit of between 90 and 180 acres, depending on local conditions; tracing it back leads to a Latin word for a kind of chariot or stagecoach, but in ancient Gaul it became the usual name for the wheeled plough. The carucate was used in the part of William the Conqueror's 1086 *Domesday Book* that catalogued the old Danelaw, together with the **bovate** (Latin *bos*, ox), which was the amount that one ox could plough in a year, so making it one-eighth of a carucate. Sometimes even this unit was too large: in Stanford in Bedfordshire the *Domesday Book* records land for half an ox, which sounds like an anatomical absurdity, but just means it was a parcel one-sixteenth of a carucate.

Much later, the **chain**, four poles long or 22 yards—the length of a cricket pitch—was introduced as a surveying tool, at first under the name **Gunter's chain**, after the famous English mathematician Edmund Gunter (1581–1626); the chain has 100 **links**, each of which is therefore 7.92 inches (Americans later and sensibly rationalized this to ten-inch links). Mr Gunter's fame spread such that nineteenth-century Americans would use "according to Gunter" as a benchmark of accuracy, as the British would say that something was "according to Hoyle". (The latter was originally a card-players' term, since Edmond Hoyle's *Short Treatise on the Game of Whist*, published in 1742, remained the standard rules until 1864, and his other works—on backgammon, piquet, quadrille, and brag—made his name synonymous with an authority on card games and later one on any subject.)

Many lesser measurements were based on parts of the body. The **foot** is an obvious example; so is the **inch**, strictly one twelfth of a foot (Latin *uncia*, twelfth part) but which was often taken to be the width of the last digit of the thumb (it was also at times taken to be the width of three "dry and round" grains of barley, **barleycorns**). A **finger breadth** is obvious, as is the **palm**, by convention either three or four inches (later, as the **handsbreath** and then the **hand** of four inches, a measurement of the height of horses). If you hold your hand with the thumb stretched out as wide as it will go, the distance from the tip of the thumb to the opposite side of the palm is roughly six inches, or a **shaftment** (the *shaft* here is probably the stuck-out thumb); two side by side made what was called in medieval Latin the **pes manualis**, the "foot of the hand".

The **cubit** (Latin *cubitum*) was the distance from the elbow to the fingertips, roughly 18 inches. It's best known from biblical references. Noah's ark was specified in Genesis:

> The length of the ark shall be three hundred
> cubits, the breadth of it fifty cubits, and the
> height of it thirty cubits.

That made it about 450 feet or 140 metres long, not too large a vessel for all the animals Noah had to pack into it. The distance from the shoulder to the wrist is about 22–23 inches, the oldest way to define an **ell**, once the usual measure in Europe for woollen cloth. (In Old English, *ell* meant the arm, so that the *elbow* is the "arm bend".) There was even a saying, *give him an inch and he will take an ell*; when the ell was replaced by the yard, the saying changed. In medieval England, the ell was fixed in size by various acts of Parliament to be 45 inches—twice the size of the older unit.

The old names for solid and liquid measures were often equally obscure and complicated. In the *Spectator* of 23 May 1711 appears a satirical note about a fictional body called the Everlasting Club:

> It appears by their Books in general, that, since
> their first Institution, they have smoked fifty Tun
> of Tobacco; drank thirty thousand Butts of Ale,
> One thousand Hogsheads of Red Port, Two
> hundred Barrels of Brandy, and a Kilderkin of
> small Beer.

At this time, most commodities were transported in wooden

casks. It would have been clearly understood among wine-makers, brewers and cidermakers that only a tyro would refer to them generically as barrels, because a **barrel** (medieval Latin *barriclus*, a small cask) was a vessel for wine or beer of a specific size that in modern British measure is 36 imperial gallons. In other industries, countries and periods, barrels have often been of other sizes—a barrel of crude oil, for example, is 35 imperial gallons or almost exactly 159 litres; the US gallon is smaller, perpetuating an older English gallon measure, so the same barrel of oil measures 42 US gallons. Incidentally, **gallon** is from the medieval Latin *galleta or galletum* for a pail or similar liquid measure, possibly of Celtic origin.

For bigger amounts, one might have **butts** (Old French *bot*, from late Latin *buttis*, a cask or wineskin), which I mentioned when describing the old-time big house and its buttery, or **pipes**, strictly of 108 and 105 imperial gallons respectively, though they were often confused; pipes were usually taller and thinner, more pipe-shaped, in fact (they're the same word, though the cask sense is older). The **tun** was about twice the size, 208 gallons; its name might be from Irish Gaelic *tonn*, a hide or skin, so the original sense might likewise have been 'wine-skin'. Other big casks were **hogsheads** of 54 gallons (definitely from *hog* + *head*, though nobody knows how pigs got involved), and **puncheons** (a name equally of uncertain origin), which varied from 72 to 120 gallons and were known in Britain mainly because

American whiskey was imported in them (and which were snapped up by farm cidermakers to add pizzazz to their brews). A **tertian** (Latin *tertius*, third) was about the same size as a puncheon, so called because it was a third of a tun.

Dropping down in size, a **kilderkin** (from Middle Dutch *kinderkin*) was half the size of a barrel; the **firkin** (from medieval Dutch meaning "a (little) fourth", that is, a quarter of a barrel) was half again, or nine gallons; half again still was the **pin** of 4½ gallons. Among other containers were the **runlet**, **rundlet**, or **roundlet** (from an Old French word meaning a small round vessel), which varied in size from three gallons up to some 18, the **cag** or **keg** (Old Norse *kaggi*, cask), a small container of less than ten gallons, and the **anker** (also from Dutch), holding about eight gallons. Those farm workers who took ale or cider out to the fields with them might do so in a **wooden bottle**, which posh people called a **costrel**, a name that could be from Old French *coste*, basket or pannier, but may instead be from *costier*, "by the side", because they were often hung on the belt.

Pub measures were necessarily smaller still. A West Country song, the *Barley Mow*, was once a favourite at the celebrations that followed the completion of the barley harvest. An early verse in some versions is this:

> We'll drink it out of the nipperkin, boys,
> Here's a health to the barley-mow!

> The nipperkin and the jolly brown bowl,
> Here's a health to the barley-mow, my brave boys,
> Here's a health to the barley-mow!

There's some confusion about the size of a **nipperkin** (from a Dutch word related to the German and Dutch verbs *nippen*, to sip), but it's usually taken to be one-eighth of an English pint. The song agrees with that, as each verse doubles up on the one before, and the sequence goes *nipperkin,* •**gill** (or **jill**, a quarter-pint, from late Latin *gillo*, water pot), *half-pint, pint*, and *quart*; it continues through **pottle** (a half gallon, from an Old French word *potel* meaning a little pot) to *gallon*, and then to the bigger measures I've already mentioned, including the *anker, hogshead*, and *pipe* (it gets very silly at the end, mentioning wells, rivers, and oceans). A *nip* of spirits is an abbreviation of *nipperkin*, in the looser sense of any small quantity.

"Do not," says the old proverb, whose sense is echoed in St Matthew's Gospel, "hide your light under a bushel." A Scots proverb warns that you "should eat a peck of salt with a man before you choose him as a friend". And the tongue-twister has it that "Peter Piper picked a peck of pickled pepper." Both **bushel** and **peck** are measures of capacity for solid goods. They turn up most commonly in references to measuring out wheat, barley, and oats, but in fact they were used for a wide range of items, including peas, beans, tomatoes, apples, pears, flour, oatmeal, salt, and linseed (a recipe book of 1919 has the instruction "Wash one peck of dandelions"). *Bushel* is from Old French *boissel*, perhaps from a word meaning a box; *peck* was originally used as a measure of oats for horses and comes from Anglo-Norman French *pek*. Sizes varied, but a bushel held about eight imperial gallons and a peck was a quarter of a bushel.

Most English cities had a standard set of measures to prevent fraud. One from Beverley in 1423 included the **modius**, a survival of the name of an ancient Roman grain measure, but by then roughly the same capacity as a bushel. Roman measures were once common—the *Anglo-Saxon Chronicle* reported bitterly in 1039 that "On this same year the sester of wheat went up to fifty-five pence, and even further", a **sester** then being about eight bushels.

Another measure once common, because it was used for coal, was the **chaldron** or **chalder** of 32 bushels or 2,000 pounds' weight (from Old French *chauderon*, kettle, ultimately from Latin *calidus*, hot). It was equivalent to four **quarters**, whose name may come from its being a quarter of a man's load. A **keel** (a shipload, in other words) was 20 chalders. In *The Monastery*, by Sir Walter Scott, appears a comment on the wealth of the monastery:

> It is said to have possessed nearly two thousand
> pounds in yearly money-rent, fourteen chalders
> and nine bolls of wheat, fifty-six chalders five

> bolls barley, forty-four chalders and ten bolls
> oats ...

A **boll** (possibly from Old Norse *bolli*, bowl) was a Scots measure that varied in size over time between two and six bushels.

There were once dozens of others, such as the **maund** (originally a Germanic word for a basket) of two or three pecks; the **fatt** of eight heaped bushels (from an Old Norse word for a vessel from which we also get *vat*); the **frundel**, a quarter of a bushel (from the Old English *farthingdeal*, a fourth part, *farthing* surviving into recent times as the name for the coin valued at one-quarter of an old penny); and the **curnock** or **crannock** (possibly from a Welsh word meaning a heap) which was once used as a dry measure in Wales, the west of England, and Ireland but varied wildly between four and fifteen bushels in various places.

Dozens (via French from Latin *duodecim*, twelve) for counts of twelve and **scores** for counts of twenty (from Old English *scoru*, a set of twenty, in turn from Old Norse *skor*, a notch, a tally, or twenty) are still familiar to many of us, but what of a **dicker** or a **shock**? A *dicker* in medieval Britain was a count of ten, a word from an ancient Germanic source (in *Domesday Book*, a dicker of iron was taken to be ten rods, each sufficient to make two horseshoes). *Shock* was perhaps from Middle Dutch or Middle Low German *schok*, of unknown origin but meaning a crowd or multitude; it was a count of sixty. It's the same word as in the agricultural sense of a stack of sheaves of corn piled up endwise to be dried; in number this varied a lot from place to place but was often ten or a dozen.

Other number words included the **flock** or **timber**, usually forty of something. This was common in the fur trade and lasted almost to modern times (the *Westminster Gazette* noted in 1901: "Ten years ago…ermine…cost 28s. to 30s. per timber of forty skins"). There were also the **great hundred**, which was six score or ten dozen (120); the **gross** of 12 dozen or 144 (from the French phrase *grosse douzaine*, literally "large dozen"), and the **great gross** of 1728, or 12 ordinary gross.

For herrings the **cade** (Latin *cadus*, a large earthenware vessel) was common; this was a barrel holding 36 score fish, 720 in total, though later it was rounded down to 500. A **last** might at times have been a measure of weight, capacity, or quantity (it's from a Germanic word meaning a load) but seems often to have been equated with the number 12, so a last of hides was 12 dozen, or 12 barrels of cod or herrings, though there are customs records of a last of codlings being a count of 496 in number and of sprats or herrings being 12,000; did anybody ever actually count them all?

We still use the **stone** in Britain, meaning 14 pounds, though only as a convenient way to measure a person's weight. It's the same word as the one meaning a rock, because the first

stone-weights were made of stone; it's from Old English *stān*, of Germanic origin. This is one of a set of ancient weights used for a variety of commodities, including coal, butter, cheese, and salt, but particularly wool. Between the pound and the stone lay the **nail** or **clove** (Latin *clovis*, nail; both were at one time used as linear measures, one-sixteenth of a yard, though how that came about or relates to the weight is unknown) of either seven or eight pounds (the latter was also called a **butcher's stone**). Two stones made a **tod** (from a Germanic word meaning a bundle); the *Edinburgh Advertiser* noted in September 1809 that

> Mr. Grant, a well known breeder of rams at Wyham
> in Lincolnshire, says that he last week clipped
> 4500 sheep, which produced 1330 tods of wool.

Thirteen stones or 182 pounds (oddly, 6½ tods) made up one **wey** or **weigh** (the same as our verb *to weigh*). An even larger amount was the **sarplier** or **sarpler** (from an Old French word for a packing-cloth), a large sack of coarse canvas for wool, which in formal measure has sometimes been said to be 26 tods and sometimes 80, a difference of some concern to the buyer, one might think.

Among the officials whose job it was to control weights and measures, one of the least enviable was the **alnager**, whose name comes from Old French *aulne*, to measure by the ell. The alnager's job in medieval times was to prevent merchants defrauding the buyers of woollen cloth (a key English export of the period) by measuring and stamping each piece to show that it conformed to the legal size. Sometimes the job that we would more recently have called an inspector of weights and measures went by that of **assizer**, because his job was to enforce the rulings of the legal *assizes* (from Old French *asseeir*, to sit, as of a court) that fixed sizes and prices. Another inspection job was that of **gauger**, literally a person who *gauges*, or measures, something; he was an exciseman or exciseman's assistant who had the job of measuring the capacity of casks containing alcohol. A related job, which involved testing the quality of ale or beer, was that of **ale-conner** mentioned earlier.

In medieval times, the **tron** or **trona** (ultimately from a Greek word for a balance or scales) was a town's public weighing machine, a pair of scales or a weigh-beam, sometimes called the King's Tron or the King's Beam. The Tron kirks in both Edinburgh and Glasgow are so named because they stood near the towns' trons. A much smaller hand-balance of the period was the **auncel**, whose name comes from the Italian *lancella*, a little balance, with the initial letter lost.

Can you hear me, mother?

PEOPLE HAVE BEEN SIGNALLING by every means conceivable—whistling, yodelling, waving their arms, flags, lamps—for as long as anybody can discover. But the history of attempts to communicate over long distances are full of words that evoke no more than puzzled looks these days.

Sandy Powell created the catchphrase of this chapter title in the early 1930s when he was performing on what people then called the **wireless**, a word that later almost vanished from the British vocabulary (Americans never did adopt it) but which has recently been adopted to describe various kinds of computer wizardry that do indeed work without wires.

By that time, only a few people still listened on **crystal sets**, in which a natural or artificial crystal was tickled by a thin wire called a **cat's whisker** into converting radio waves into speech and music that was halfway intelligible wearing headphones in a quiet room. Most by then were using sets that incorporated **valves** (**vacuum tubes** in the US) to amplify the sound, getting their power from a **high-tension battery** (which supplied a high voltage) and an **accumulator** (the source of the low voltage to heat the filaments in the valves), a lead-acid battery that you took to the local radio shop each week to get recharged. Early valve sets were unstable and if you tried to coax one into working better it could easily turn into a transmitter and kill reception for your neighbours. Peter Eckersley, the BBC's first chief engineer, used to go on the air and beg listeners not to do this:

Please don't oscillate. It's not British!

The modern story of communications begins with a man called Claude Chappe in revolutionary France in the early 1790s, who created what a classically educated friend suggested he call the *télégraphe* (Greek *tele*, far off + *graphos*, something that writes). It was a type of **semaphore** (from another French word of slightly later date that was to be borrowed from Greek *sēma*, sign + *-phoros*, bearer) that consisted of a pair of rotatable arms on a crosspiece, supported on a mast. The French government adopted it as a way to get military and naval intelligence to Paris much more quickly than by the only alternative, a man on a horse. The first line started working in May 1794. The British Navy immediately took over the idea and erected lines of these **telegraph** stations to communicate with Dover, Portsmouth,

Plymouth and other key ports. The British system employed a frame of six shutters, black on one side, white on the other, designed by a clergyman named George Murray. By the 1830s, there were networks of these stations in Europe and other countries.

It was in the 1830s that inventors such as Samuel Morse in the US and William Cook and Charles Wheatstone in the UK harnessed the new-fangled electricity to similar ends, creating thereby the **electric telegraph**. Though it was given that name to distinguish it from the older mechanical system, within a few years the latter was obsolete and anyone speaking of the telegraph meant only the electrical type. Morse's system employed a code of short and long pulses (dots and dashes), the **Morse code**, which is now almost as obsolete as the telegraph itself. The telegraph was the primary means of long-distance communication for many decades, though to call the result a **telegraphic communication** or **telegraphic dispatch** was cumbersome; by about 1855 **telegram** (Greek *gramma*, a thing written) had come into general use, though some argued unsuccessfully against it, as the eminent classical Greek scholar Richard Shilleto did in a letter to the *Times* in October 1857:

> May I suggest to such as are not contented with 'Telegraphic Despatch' the rightly constructed word 'telegrapheme'? ... I protest against such a barbarism as 'telegram'.

A decade later, Mr Shilleto would presumably also have made adverse comment concerning **cablegram** for a telegram sent through one of the new undersea cables. Indeed some did, on the grounds that it was a bastard offspring of Greek and English, and argued it should be **calogram**, from the Greek *kalos*, cable. Nobody took any notice, perhaps because most people shortened it to **cable**. Similar objections were made later about **television**—C P Scott, editor of the *Manchester Guardian*, is reputed to have argued:

> Television? The word is half Greek, half Latin. No good can come of it.

Inventors improved the telegraph with devices such as the **telautograph**, in which writing or drawing at the transmitting end was reproduced at the other, a sort of primitive fax machine that was widely used for many years in the US. Another was the **phonopore** (Greek *poros*, passage), an inductive system in which telephone signals could be piggy-backed on a telegraph wire so both systems could be used at once. Combining a typewriter and a **teleprinter** (or **teletypewriter** or **teletype**) permitted a printed message to appear at the receiving end; in the 1930s one version became the **telex** system (short for *teleprinter exchange*). The telephone gradually made the telegraph obsolete, though inland telegrams lasted until 1982 in Britain (to be replaced by the **telemessage**) and Western Union closed their telegram service in the US in 2006; telex also still clings to life. As an example of linguistic conservatism, it's still common in Britain to refer to **telegraph poles** rather than **telephone poles** (from the *Daily Mirror* of 5 September 2005: "Five telegraph poles cut down in west Wales may be due to revival of the custom of testing a bridegroom with obstacles on his way to church").

As a result of the experiments of Heinrich Hertz in Berlin in the 1880s on what were at first called **Hertzian waves**, people began to think of using them to communicate with. Edison was in there very early and actually took out a patent in 1891, though his widely-reported boast to the US press in 1887 was a bit premature:

> Thomas A. Edison has returned from Florida with
> the results of his wireless telegraphic
> experiments in shape to put to practical use.

It was Marconi who famously developed the idea further. The first **radio-telegrams**, so described in the press, were received at his Cornish headquarters in 1902, though others had previously referred to the technique as **wireless telegraphy**, focusing on the key difference between the new method and the old.

The difficulty of finding pithy names for new technologies is illustrated by this report in an Illinois newspaper dated 31 December 1901:

> Marconi's wonderful invention has set the
> officials of the navy and signal service, where his

> system is in use, hunting for a new word. They are
> casting about for a short and simple term to stand
> for the laborious expression now employed: 'A
> message transmitted by wireless telegraphy.' A
> student of natural forces in the navy believes that
> 'etherogram' would be a good one. 'Aerogram' and
> 'airgram,' quite as convenient as 'telegram' and
> 'cablegram,' find much favor. 'Marconigram' has
> also been suggested by an ingenious layman.

Aerogram—a message sent through the air—had also been suggested by others but never caught on. Neither did **etherogram**, which was based on the old idea of an intangible **ether** (Greek *aither*, upper air, because it was then thought to permeate space beyond the moon) that was thought to be required for light and similar waves such as radio to pass. Back in 1885 Hertz had proved it wasn't needed, but the idea took a long time to die in everyday vocabulary and hasn't quite vanished even now. *Etherogram* was said at the time to be Marconi's preference, since he felt that **Marconigram** savoured too much of self-advertisement, but the latter won for a decade, until people started to prefer **radiogram**, short for *radio-telegram*, a quite separate word from the early home entertainment device that combined a radio with a **gramophone**.

At around the same time as these early radio experiments, the telephone was being developed for everyday use. The first automatic exchange had been opened as early as November 1891 in

Laporte, Indiana, famously by a Kansas undertaker named Almon B Strowger, who had become incensed by calls asking for him instead being put through to a competitor, whose wife was the local telephone operator or **hello girl**. Developments of Strowger's devices survived until the 1980s, with their characteristic rotating **dial** that sent the necessary electrical pulses to the equipment at the exchange (and even today we often still dial a number, though it has been quite a while since new telephones came fitted with one). Similarly, early phones had the microphone or **mouthpiece** as part of the main instrument, but the **earpiece** was separate; when you finished you **hung up** by putting the latter on a hook on the side of the phone, which also terminated the call. If you forgot, your telephone was **off the hook** and unable to receive calls.

Such automatic diallers were for many decades confined to local calls. If you wanted to call somebody in another town, the operator for the GPO (the General Post Office, who had the telephone monopoly) connected you manually as a **trunk call**. H G Wells wrote in July 1909:

> There is the usual trouble in connecting up,
> minute voices in Folkestone and Dover and
> London call to one another and are submerged by
> buzzings and throbbings.

Trunk refers to the main body, line, or route of something and had previously been used for the main course of a river and a railway main line, among other senses. It is hidden inside the abbreviation **STD**, which appeared in the 1960s for the GPO's automatic long-distance dialling system that in full was named **Subscriber Trunk Dialling**. Long-distance calls were punctuated by a *pip-pip-pip* to mark that another three minutes had passed (as a radio producer in the 1960s I had to ask the telephone operator for a **pipless** call to silence the **pips** when recording an interview by telephone). Readers of mature years will recall the old red telephone boxes containing what we would now call a payphone, with their equipment finished in black stove enamel; the device was furnished with two buttons, **Button A** for connecting your call and taking your money and **Button B** for getting it back if your call failed and the equipment was feeling charitable.

Even before broadcasting began, it was possible to sit at home and listen to concerts, West End plays, and religious services through the medium of the **Electrophone** ("Song, Mirth and Music By Wire to your Home", for £5 a year), which operated from 1895 but is now completely forgotten. Microphones were connected via telephones to multiple subscribers, who could even get a crude form of stereo. It featured briefly in a story, *The Assyrian Rejuvenator* by Clifford Ashdown, published in *Cassell's Magazine* in 1902:

> Mr Rodney Pringle had secured his favourite seat
> … and in the intervals of feeding listened to a

> selection from Mascagni through a convenient
> electrophone, price sixpence in the slot.

The service closed in 1926, rendered obsolete by the upstart wireless, joining a long list that have been surpassed by new technologies.

Going, going ... gone?

AS PREVIOUS CHAPTERS have illustrated, technology has been a powerful driver of vocabulary change in the past century.

Computers, as a prominent example, have supplanted the once-ubiquitous **typewriter**, in the process displacing **carbon paper**, something its former users will scarcely regret. Few writers now create handwritten manuscripts using **fountain pens**, let alone **steel-nibbed pens** that required **inkwells** and replacement **pen nibs**; without liquid ink, **blotting paper** is now a rarity. Come to that, who now speaks of **pen wipers**, **writing desks**, or **pen holders**? Cheap digital calculators mean that the **ready reckoner**, **slide rule**, **adding machine**, **logarithms** or **log tables**, and the **comptometer** (the proprietary name of a type of calculating-machine) are now—for the most part—museum pieces.

Those words "for the most part" have been included to mollify readers who are thinking to themselves that *they* still use fountain pens, or that *their* slide rule was still handy for dashing off quick-and-dirty calculations, or that a typewriter still had pride of place in *their* office. That, of course, is the problem with discussing the vanishing vocabulary of the past century. When writing about the 1700s or 1800s, distance gives enough perspective to be sure that words really have left our active vocabularies. With the twentieth century, such certainties evaporate.

In entertainment, **bioscope** is a century out of date as a name for what we now call the *cinema* or the *movies*, as has the fuller original form of that last word, **moving pictures**; several generations have passed since we had cause to specify that wonder of the age, the **talkies** that supplanted silent films; within a decade or so, **picture house** had also gone and **the pictures** has followed. **Cinema organs** no longer rise from hidden depths to entertain us in the intervals between films, not least because there's no need for intervals now that film programmes consist of only a **main feature**, with no supporting **B-feature** or **second feature** or weekly **newsreel**. The idea of **continuous performance**, in which some patrons happily started watching a film in the middle, strikes us now as bizarre. Even the longest film no longer comes complete with an inbuilt **intermission** for those with weak bladders or faltering attention spans or to allow the **usherettes** to sell ice cream.

Interestingly, **gramophone** has had something of a revival in recent years (though, to judge from a recent small ad in *The Age* in Melbourne, which claimed to be auctioning "grammar phones", it's not universally known among telephone copy-takers). However, **record player** is pretty much defunct, as are the **autochangers** that allowed a sequence of vinyl discs to be played without human intervention. DJs in clubs still like their **vinyl** (and firms still press them) because they permit presentation tricks impossible with CDs, but for the general public they're exotic survivals. Gone with them is the vocabulary of **33⅓**, **45** and **78 rpm**, **EP** (extended-play), and **LP** (long-play) discs. The idea that you played a 78 rpm shellac disc with a replaceable gramophone needle, and could choose bamboo for a soft sound or steel for a crisper one, is halfway to alchemy today. Since we no longer have such fragile reproduction mechanisms, the simile comparing somebody to a **broken record** when they keep repeating the same trite thoughts, like a needle stuck in a groove, has lost its link to real life. Also gone are the **radiograms** that combined a record player with a wireless. And who now remembers the **quadraphonic** sound of the 1970s, that long-abandoned attempt to create a surround-sound ambience? When we can carry thousands of audio tracks in a device the size of a pack of playing cards, the idea of a bulky **tape recorder** that needed reels of magnetic tape to be loaded and threaded before you could play it sounds unbearably clumsy. That a predecessor, the **wire recorder**, required reels of iron wire to do the same job sounds now almost extraordinary; an example of the early 1930s was called the **Blattnerphone**, and another, the **Marconi-Stille recorder**, was still in use by broadcasting organizations as late as the 1950s, though it spun metal tape at a lethal 850 feet a minute and each tape reel weighed 21 pounds.

Another area in which technological innovation has wrought a revolution is the kitchen. For most people, refrigerators have long since put paid to the **meat safe** and the ventilated **pantry**. Washing machines have eased the labour of the weekly **washday**—no longer is it a matter of scrubbing clothes on a **washboard** in a **dolly tub** full of hot water, pressing the clothes down to immerse and stir them with a **dolly stick** (*dolly* here probably comes from the fanciful idea that the dolly stick, with its long stick and protruding arms and feet, looked like a child's doll). If you had one, you would instead boil the clothes in a **copper** while stirring them with a wooden **copper stick**, then putting them through a **mangle** or **wringer** to remove the excess water before putting them out on the **clothes line**—with a **clothes pole** to lift the rope and clothes clear of the ground—or hanging them on the **clothes horse** before an open fire. No wonder mothers were tired at the end of Monday's weekly washday.

Speaking of open fires: though country people still enjoy them, for most urban people they have been replaced by central heating, to the extent that some city children have no idea what coal looks like, or indeed where it comes from. And so another set of words drifts towards the vanishing point: **coal cellar**, **coal hole**, **coal scuttle**, and the **coalman** with his horse and cart and weekly delivery, as well as **fireirons**, **toasting forks**, **chimney sweeps**, and especially (and thankfully) **chimney fires**.

Not only the coalman has gone from our street, but so has the **rag-and-bone man** and his horse and cart, collecting unwanted items in the hope of a small profit. **Trams** have almost entirely vanished (though in some cities a high-tech update has re-appeared), and so have **trolley buses**, whose long arms for collecting power from overhead cables seemed regularly to become dislodged at the most inconvenient moments, requiring the bus conductor to haul out a long bamboo pole from under the bus to reattach it. Come to that, **bus conductors** have now almost entirely gone, an expensive luxury. With the maturing of the technology of the car, **chokes** and **starting handles** are obsolete, the notice **Running in—please pass** is now never seen, few vehicles have **running boards**, and none now have that odd extra fold-away outside seat at the back called in Britain a **dicky** (probably from *Richard*, applied to a servant who sat in its predecessor in a horse-drawn carriage) and in the US a **rumble seat** (because you suffered all the vibration of the road).

We can be sure that words attached to a specific event like the Second World War have gone from everybody's active vocabulary. Unless you're a historian of the period, or of senior years, or spend much time gossiping with aged relatives, it's unlikely that you will need to speak of **ARP** (air-raid precautions), **air-raid shelters**, **Anderson shelters** (a type of shelter named after the Home Secretary of 1939-40, Sir John Anderson), **ration books** and **clothing coupons**, **gasmasks**, **utility furniture**, **egg powder**, **barrage balloons**, **V-1 flying bombs** (or **doodlebugs**) and **V-2 rockets**, **bomb sites**, **CC41** (*Civilian Clothing 1941*, despite its name a specification that also appeared on furniture, housewares, and other items), **spivs**, and **demob suits** (which *demobilized* ex-servicemen were provided with on their return to **civvy street**). Such terms, thankfully, lost their active associations either with the cessation of hostilities or—in the case of rationing—in the decade that followed.

Epilogue

Words that never made it

WE CONTINUE to invent new words—not least because there are so many new things that need names—to such an extent that we are living through, or perhaps enduring, one of the most prolific phases of word creation in the history of English. Such creativity has not always been welcomed.

Ben Jonson wrote in 1640 that

> A man coynes not a new word without some perill; and less fruit; for if it happen to be received, the praise is but moderate; if refus'd, the scorn is assur'd.

In the nineteenth century, the creation of new words was considered an uncivil affront to readers. Robert Graves, in *Goodbye to All That* of 1929, recorded that Thomas Hardy once told him,

> Once or twice recently he had looked up a word in
> the dictionary for fear of being again accused of
> coining.

A much earlier period of word creation—in the sixteenth and
seventeenth centuries—attracted even greater critical oppro-
brium. Many writers were known for inventing new words
based on Latin. Furious opponents argued that such arcane
constructions were diluting the native splendour of what was
then still considered a Germanic language, though few appre-
ciated just how many Latin words had by then found their way
into English via French. Such words came to be known as **inkhorn terms**, **inkhorn** being an old term meaning an inkwell, since
early examples were made from a cow's horn. The derisory
implication was either that such words needed too much ink
to write them, or that they appeared as though from the ink itself
(**smelling of the inkhorn** meant pedantic writing). Much of the
criticism was unfair, since English needed more words: during
the period of the Renaissance, activities of all sorts broadened as
a result of a new spirit of inquiry and exploration and English
vocabulary needed to enlarge to cope with it.

Shakespeare, for example, was a great creator of words, perhaps a
thousand of which we still use today, such as *circumstantial, dis-
content, eventful, frugal, grovel, laughable, monumental, pedant, reclusive,* and
stealthy. It was inevitable in a period of linguistic inventiveness
that some of his new words would catch on while others failed to

gain public acceptance, such as **adoptious** (connected with adoption); **bubukle** (a humorous conflation of *bubo* and *carbuncle*); **cadent** (falling, from Latin *cadere*, to fall); **exsufflicate** (describing language that is windy or overblown, from Latin *exsufflare*, to blow out or away); **forgetive** (possibly from *forge* and perhaps meaning that a person is capable of inventive thought—nothing to do with *forget*); **immoment** (trifling, from *moment*); **irregulous** (lawless or disorderly, from Latin *regula*, rule); **nuthook** (a sheriff's deputy, previously a hooked stick used to pull down branches when harvesting nuts); and **oppugnancy** (the state of being *oppugnant*, opposing or antagonistic, from Latin *oppugnantia*).

In his creativity, Shakespeare was in tune with his times, because other playwrights of the period were likewise expanding the language. They all mixed their hits with misses. Take John Marston, a contemporary, who was particularly known for his extravagantly inventive vocabulary. He created **bause** (to kiss); **extracture** (something extracted); **gargalize** (to gargle); **incomprehense** (boundless or unlimited); **mangonist** (one who sells inferior wares, from Latin *mango*, a dealer in refurbished goods); and the magnificent **catastrophonical** (which has no meaning at all, so far as anyone can tell).

Other writers tried **arrosion** (the action of gnawing, from Latin *arrodere*, to gnaw or nibble); **baggagery** (worthless rabble);

bribage (the extraction of illegal fees by officials); **collachrymate** (accompanied by weeping, from Latin *col-*, together + *lacrimare*, to shed tears); **illecebrous** (alluring, enticing, or attractive, from Latin *illicere*, to entice); **jolliment** (merriment or jollity); **labascency** (the state of moving in an unsteady way, from Latin *labascere*, to be tottery); **malt-worm** (a drunkard); **oblivionize** (to consign to oblivion); **pastinaceous** (relating to the parsnip, from Latin *pastinaca*, parsnip); **refriscative** (refreshing, from Latin *refriscare*, to refresh); **sparrow-blasted** (thunderstruck or dumbfounded); **suppeditate** (subdued, overcome, from Latin *suppeditare*, to overthrow); and **ventilow** (a fan).

It's unfair to castigate these writers in particular, since the number of words created throughout history that have never gained popular approval is very large. If you search the CD-ROM of *Oxford English Dictionary* for all the words and senses marked both as "obsolete" and "rare", 22,889 results come back, ranging from **aback** (a square tablet or compartment, a word used just once, by Ben Jonson in a play of 1603) to **zygostat** (which one of the two writers of the seventeenth century that mentioned it defined as a person appointed to check the weights and measures in a market, while the other said it was a balance used by jewellers; either way it's from Greek *zygon*, a balance beam + *statikē*, the science of weighing).

Dr Johnson's famous *Dictionary* of 1755 contained many

such rarities, which his readers bitterly complained about. **Effumability**, for example, meaning the ability to be converted into vapour (from Latin *fumus*, smoke) is known to have been used only once, by Robert Boyle in his *Sceptical Chymist* of 1680; a **shapesmith** was "one who undertakes to improve the form of the body", a little gem of misleading humorous definition for a person whom the *Oxford English Dictionary* makes clear was more commonly called a corset-maker; an **amatorculist** was "a little insignificant lover; a pretender to affection", from Latin *amatorculus*, a pitiful lover; **bedswerver** hardly needs to be glossed as a bed-hopper, an unfaithful spouse; to be **subderisorious** was to be "scoffing or ridiculing with tenderness and delicacy", a difficult art; something or someone that was **bicipitous** (Latin *bi-*, two + *caput*, head) had two heads—Johnson took the word from a work of the physician Sir Thomas Browne, the only person known to have used it; another from the same source and equally rare was **latirostrous**, broad-beaked, which Browne created from Latin *latus*, broad + *rostrum*, beak.

Browne is graced and immortalized in the *Oxford English Dictionary* by 3,793 citations altogether, which include many rarities that he created, including **aculeous** (needle-like, from Latin *acūleus*, a sting); **cenatory** (relating to dinner, from Latin *cenatorious*); **elychnious** (of the nature of a wick, from Greek *en*, in + *lychnos*, lamp); **hypenemy** (a *wind-egg*, an imperfect or addled egg, from the ancient superstition that a hen that laid such an egg had been impregnated by the wind, from Greek *hupo*, beneath + *anemos*, wind); **ingannation** (deception, from Latin *inganno*, fraud); **laqueary** (armed with a noose to entangle his opponent, like a Roman gladiator, from Latin *laqueus*, noose); **nasicornous** (having a horn on the nose, from Latin *nāsus*, nose + *cornū*, horn); **paleous** (of the nature of chaff, from Latin *palea*, chaff); **stillicidious** (produced by falling in drops, from Latin *stilla*, a drop + a form of *cadere*, to fall); and **zodiographer** (a person who writes about animals, from Greek *zōion*, animal + *graphein*, to write).

Though people have never ceased creating new words, another period of especially extravagant word-coining took place in the US in the early decades of the nineteenth century, matching the exuberance of the period. The nineteenth-century American grammarian William Fowler feared that as English spread across the continent, people would "break loose from the laws of language". Something like that actually happened, and no grammarian or schoolmaster had the power to stop it.

To **absquatulate**, for example, meant to decamp or leave, probably based on a mixture of *abscond* and *squat*, with a Latinate ending borrowed from words like *perambulate*. It was common enough that it became one of the favourite *bêtes noires* of writers on style in the latter part of the century, such as Walton Burgess, who wrote *Five Hundred Mistakes of Daily Occurrence in Speaking*

Pronouncing and Writing the English Language, Corrected, a title sufficient in itself to make the strongest quail. He included *absquatulate* in a list of those to avoid, with this example of it in action:

> He has absquatulated, and taken the specie with
> him.

He remarked disdainfully that "'absconded' is a more classical word". Indeed, but who cared about the classics?

Absquatulate is still common enough to be found in some dictionaries, as is **honey-fuggle**, to deceive or obtain by deception. Other fanciful terms from the same stable include **hornswoggle**, to cheat or swindle, and **snollygoster**, a shrewd and unprincipled person, especially a politician. The editor of the *Columbus Dispatch* of October 1895 noted,

> A Georgia editor kindly explains that "a
> snollygoster is a fellow who wants office,
> regardless of party, platform or principles, and
> who, whenever he wins, gets there by the sheer
> force of monumental talknophical assumnacy".

Talknophical assumnacy: two words that encapsulate an entire cigar-chewing, bear-wrestling, tall-talking century. To **bloviate** was to talk pompously; US president Warren Gamaliel Harding used it a lot and was by all accounts the classic example of somebody who orates windily and verbosely. It's a compound of *blow*, in its sense of boasting (also in another typical Americanism, *blowhard*), with a mock-Latin ending to give it the self-important stature implicit in its meaning.

Savagerous was popular for a long while, formed as a blend of *savage* and *dangerous* (first recorded by Frances Trollope in her *Domestic Manners of the Americans* in 1831). A **sockdolager** was a heavy blow, possibly combining *sock*, meaning to give somebody a blow, with *doxology*, the little hymn of praise sung towards the end of a church service (which also gave rise to the long-dead verb **doxologize**, to say the doxology). The particular claim to fame of *sockdolager* is that its related verb was virtually the last word President Lincoln ever heard. In Tom Taylor's play *Our American Cousin*, there occurs the line "Well, I guess I know enough to turn you inside out, you sockdologizing old man-trap", and as the audience laughed, John Wilkes Booth fired the fatal shot.

Among those that had only a temporary popularity is **goshbus-tified**, which is said to mean "excessively pleased and gratified", though the only example I can find, from the *Tioga Eagle* of Pennsylvania in 1843, has the opposite sense:

> If I ever tell a city gal she is handsome again, I
> hope I may be goshbustified, chawed right up
> and spit out in small quantities.

In *Dialect Notes* in 1913, Elsie Warnock listed several extraordinary terms she had discovered, of unknown origin and meaning, such as **supergobosnoptious**, **hyperfirmatious**, and **scrumdifferous**. Others of like type include **dumfungled** (used up); **exfluncticated** or **exflunctified** (destroyed); **conbobberation** (a disturbance); **teetotaciously** (an elaborated form of *teetotal* but meaning completely or utterly); **monstracious** (excessively so); **helliferocious** (savagely untamed); and **slangwhanger** (an abusive speaker).

So now you can translate a sentence from a speech by Representative Wick of Indiana, which was reported in the *Congressional Globe* of 20 July 1840:

> The Administration is bodaciously used up,
> teetotaciously exflunctified.

Index of featured words

C

For Not to be taken
from the room.
reference